Be a good in the world

365 Days of Good Deeds, Inspired
Ideas and Acts of Kindness

Brenda Knight

MJF BOOKS

New York

Published by MJF Books
Fine Communications
322 Eighth Avenue
New York, NY 10001

Be a Good in the World
LC Control Number: 2015951401
ISBN 978-1-60671-329-7

This edition is published by MJF Books in arrangement with
Viva Editions, an imprint of Start Midnight, LLC.

Printed in the United States of America.

MJF Books and the MJF colophon are trademarks of
Fine Creative Media, Inc.

QF   10   9   8   7   6   5   4   3   2   1

This is for Richard J. Chin, who shows me each and every day how to be a best in the world, and how tolerance teaches us all about love. I also dedicate this book to my mother Helen and my sisters Martha and Lola Kay. They are shining examples of kindness, generosity, and caring. My nephew Brian, aka "Brain," Reed inspires me with his huge brain and even bigger heart.

I am grateful for you all. Big love.

We make a living by what we get, but we make a life by what we give.

—WINSTON CHURCHILL

Contents

The Power of the Human Heart

When I was working on the Random Acts of Kindness campaign, it was an incredibly joy-filled work experience. I usually do love what I do but this took it to a whole new level. My work was not just about helping my company or paying my rent for the month—it suddenly really meant something. We were making the world a better place, one act of kindness at a time. There was electricity in the air and we arrived at work each day to see what miracles had happened overnight while we were sleeping.

I remember the first day we knew everything had really changed; we found out through the US postal service. Usually we only had a dozen or so pieces of mail, bills mostly and a few queries, letters from readers or an order or two. One day, the mailman knocked and said, "I need help here!" He had *bags* of letters from people all over the country and a *ton* of ones with suggestions of acts of kindness. There were tears and laughter as we sat down on the floor and tore open the envelopes, reading aloud from the letters. Some were in children's big blocky letters (these usually had the best ideas of kindness) and others in elders' careful script. I treasure that memory of seeing the power of the human heart that day.

Brenda Knight
El Cerrito, California

chapter one

January

The Month of New Beginnings

If you want happiness for an hour—take a nap. If you want happiness for a day—go fishing. If you want happiness for a year—inherit a fortune. If you want happiness for a lifetime—help someone else.

—CHINESE PROVERB

January 1:
Resolve to Be a Force for Good in This World

New Year's Day. Did you make a New Year's resolution for this year? Throw that word *resolution* out the window. It's not strong enough to hold people to their goals—or at least that is true for me and everyone I know! If you want to eat healthier, spend more time with your family, or finally volunteer at your church's soup kitchen, go ahead and make these things happen. Tell people about your mission and maybe they will join forces with you. I had so much fun at Glide Memorial Church serving lunch that my friends asked to come along with me! Or, if you want to jump-start your New Year's with a *major* act of kindness, head on down to LA for the New Year's Race for A Place Called Home (apch.org). They are a safe haven in South Central Los Angeles where underserved youth are empowered to take ownership of the quality and direction of their lives through programs in education, arts, and well-being. These young people are inspired to make a meaningful difference in their community and the world.

January 2:
Just Say Hello!

. . . .

Try something new this year and check out the Just Say Hello campaign on Oprah's website. The campaign (find it at oprah.com/health/Just-Say-Hello-How-to-Participate) encourages kindness and strives to combat loneliness by reading and connecting. A howdy-do to a stranger might make your day and a new pal in the process. I read about this excellent friendliness project in Oprah's *O Magazine* a few Sundays ago and immediately felt inspired to try it that day. My boyfriend and I went to do our weekend chores, which include buying fresh flowers from our neighborhood stand. An older gentleman was standing there smelling the roses, always a good idea in my mind. I remembered to say "Hi" as instructed by Oprah and he responded with a big smile and asked for my input on flowers for a lady friend. As you might imagine, quite a conversation ensued, and my boyfriend, who is even friendlier than I am, joined in. Soon the florist was involved and our new gentleman friend turned out to be a fascinating conversationalist. He had been a fighter pilot in the Korean War, very highly decorated, and had traveled all over the world before returning home to El Cerrito. Widowed some years back, he was only beginning to get back out there and date. After landing upon a carefully selected bouquet of red roses and pink lilies, he headed off to the dance at the senior center. I noticed he had a good bit of pep in his step and I remember having a good feeling about his first date. We kept our eyes peeled for Colonel Jarvis when in the vicinity of the flower shop, and sure enough, the next time we saw him he had pictures of his lady friend from the dance featuring a corsage he had gotten for her. Things were looking pretty swell all around and he looked pleased as punch.

So, thanks, Oprah, for another great idea!

January 3:
Earn an Advanced Degree in Giving

I count myself very lucky indeed to know the world's only Jollytologist, Allen Klein. The story of how he came to have this distinction astounds me. Ever hear of a "Jollytologist"? Well, meet Allen Klein. Through his books and his presentations, Klein shows people worldwide how to deal with everything from traffic jams to corporate culture. Klein got into this unusual line of work after his wife died of a rare liver disease at the age of 34 when he saw how humor helped her, and those around her, to cope. He now teaches others how to find humor in trying times. His audiences include people in 48 American states as well as Israel and Australia, and clients from IBM to the IRS. Comedian Jerry Lewis has said that Allen Klein is "a noble and vital force watching over the human condition." I agree with Jerry Lewis and would add that Allen Klein makes the world a better place, every day!

January 4:
Love and Lattes

. . . .

Leave a tip and a little thank-you note in the tip jar at your favorite coffee or ice cream shop. Many of us remember the days when we had to work retail or hospitality while in high school or college. The staff is working hard, so show your appreciation for your latte and their positive attitude with a dollar or two. I have put in little "good job" notes in the tip jar at my local Peet's Coffee & Tea. I think good work should be acknowledged and people should know they are appreciated (and so should their boss!). I have made lifelong friends at the two Peet's I have frequented and it is nice to see them across the counter every morning. Those relationships all began with four little words: "How are you today?"

January 5:
National Motivation and Inspiration Day

. . . .

Think about the things that motivate and inspire you. How can you inspire others? What lifts you up? Who fills you with hope and happiness? Cultivate these qualities in yourself and pay attention to who provides your "day lifters." You may be surprised!

January 6:
Do YOU

. . . .

This is your life! Only you can truly control your choices. Choosing happiness is the best way to achieve being a good to yourself as well as the world. Here are some suggestions for how you can ensure simple joy in your life:

- Be the best you can be by your own standards.
- Surround yourself with people who inspire you and make you feel good.
- Focus on what you have, not what you lack.
- Optimism trumps pessimism every time!
- Smile often and genuinely.
- Be honest, to yourself and to others.
- Help others.
- Embrace your past, live in the present, and look forward for what is yet to come.

January 7:
Scatter Joy All Around

Think about how you can create little moments of happiness for others. Help a friend plant her garden, buy an extra coffee for your coworker, pay the toll for the car behind you on the bridge, and even take your kids to a movie. All those little things can add up to *big* joy.

January 8:
Operation Gratitude

I learned about this from my mom, whose church regularly sends cards, letters, and care packages overseas to the armed forces. My mom and her fellow church ladies bake some of the best cookies in the world, so they gather up all kinds of goodies and treats and send them overseas where the taste of down home surely brings many smiles of satisfaction. Those who are less gifted in the baking department (such as *me*!) can make a $15 donation to Operation Gratitude, which pays for one care package for one serviceperson. Operation Gratitude (operationgratitude.com) has sent over a million of these kindness kits around the world!

January 9:
Be a Good on Your Own Block

Make a list of small things you can do around your house and place of work to conserve energy and water, stop waste, and increase the recycling. Then start doing them!

January 10:
Veg Out

Have you heard of "food deserts"? I certainly never did until reading last year in *The New York Times* about entire swaths of urban areas with nothing but corner stores filled with processed, packaged foods and no produce whatsoever. I started paying attention and it is true.

There is something you can do about it. By making a donation to WholesomeWave.org, they will provide fresh fruits and veggies to these underserved communities. How great is that? Actually, it is even better, as Wholesome Wave obtains their organic produce from small and mid-sized farmers.

January 11:
National Human Trafficking Awareness Day

Support Love146, an organization that provides holistic care to children who have survived exploitation, enforced labor, abuse, and even slavery. Join a task force, fundraise for abolition, spread the word, or donate to this cause at love146.org.

January 12:
Emit Good Vibes

Take stock of your day-to-day life. Are you giving to others or is there an imbalance? Do your work and your immediate family get 99% of what you offer the world? You can change that in one day. Donate more of your time or money to a charity. Supporting a cause will help keep you informed about social issues and can strengthen your sense of well being, while benefiting others in the process. Additionally, monetary donations are tax deductible, which is really just a bonus: the real reward is not just on April 15 but comes the other 364 days of the year.

January 13:
Look Up!

Put down your smartphone and make eye contact, person to person. Nowadays, I consider that a major act of kindness and courtesy, as well.

January 14:
Karma on Wheels

Slow down and let other drivers merge and go ahead of you. Allow every pedestrian to amble across the street, the slower the better. Is that extra five minutes of driving time going to ruin your life? No, but being a patient, *safe,* and nice driver will make the ride all the more pleasant and will send a ray of goodness in your wake.

January 15:
Lend an Ear

Counselors can contribute enormously to our troops when they return from their service term. I honestly think my ex-Marine dad had PTSD. Post-traumatic stress was not even acknowledged until long after the Vietnam War, and only through the hard work of many activists.

Therapists and mental health professionals can really help our military veterans by volunteering their own services through the organization Give an Hour (giveanhour.org) and this is extremely helpful to families of vets. Listening can change lives for the better in a big way.

January 16:
Love Lifts You Up

If you have frequent flier miles you are not planning to use, give them to service members who have been injured in the line of duty and need to be flown to proper medical treatment. This can also enable family members to visit them. Check out fisherhouse.org to discover all you need to know about Fisher House Foundation's Hero Miles Program. Love has an enormous power to heal, so sharing your unused miles stretches *your* love a mighty long way!

January 17:
What the World Needs Now

Tell someone close to you how much you love them, even if you're sure they already know.

January 18:
Cook It Forward

. . . .

If you love to cook and love to help people, this might be the option for you: teach cooking classes or offer your services as a free guide to getting the healthiest groceries at the best prices via Cooking Matters, a division of Share Our Strength. What I love about this is that it is both personal and oh-so-practical. CookingMatters.org pairs you up with a local group. You can bake up a lot of love while showing others how to do the same.

January 19:
Uncommon Courtesy

. . . .

Make a point of smiling at everyone you encounter and cross paths with today. Such a simple thing can mean an awful lot.

January 20:
Dr. Martin Luther King, Jr. Day of Service

. . . .

Life's most persistent and urgent question is,
"What are you doing for others?"

—DR. MARTIN LUTHER KING, JR.

Thanks to *Selma*, a new generation of moviegoers is learning about the man who fought for civil rights, justice, and dignity for African Americans. Along with Bayard Rustin, John Lewis, and other activists, Dr. King appealed to the best within us all. Find a project in your community or register your own project through mlkday. gov. Many presidents share a legal holiday in February, but courageous Dr. King gets his own day.

January 21:
Share Your Skills

. . . .

Teach someone a craft or skill you are good at. Sharing your talent with someone else may allow them to discover their own potential. Whether it's cooking, archery, or photography, spend some time doing what you love with another. Teaching people how to do something new will help you maintain your interest and establish a connection with the person you are with. No doubt you will learn just as much from being a teacher.

January 22:
Only Connect

Be a mentor to someone. Everyone needs help to achieve their dreams and goals in life. Mentorship is an excellent way of providing needed help, encouragement, and guidance. Look for opportunities to mentor people at virtuefirst.org/virtues/service.

January 23:
Give Away Your Old Stuff

I've said it before and I'll say it again: we all have too much stuff. Do a favor for people in need and give away some of the things you no longer use or wear. Others would be happy to have them and you will simplify your life and enjoy your time more. Find a few locations that you can drop off your stuff or call an organization that collects goods to redistribute to those in need. There are Goodwills or Salvation Army centers in every town, large or small, so you can donate to help others.

January 24:
Foster a Four-Legger

If you are a parent of young children, you probably hear a steady chorus of requests for a dog. You can find out if dog ownership is right for your family by checking out guidedogs.com and applying to raise a puppy for the blind. What a wonderful way to experiment and do good! This is an excellent demonstration of responsible behavior that will doubtless leave a lasting imprint upon your children.

January 25:
Have Mercy

. . . .

Donate a gift through Mercy Corps. It's as simple as this: choose a gift on their website. The recipient gets a card that explains the gift and donation made in their name, and your gift helps families in need. Visit gifts.mercycorps.org to view the gift selection, ranging from clean water to a goat. You can choose to remain anonymous or you can personalize with a friendly note to a family on another part of the globe. It's really nice to see how your gift is of benefit and people have developed long-distance friendships through this kindly organization. Often, the daily headlines are reflected by the regions presented. Currently, families affected by Ebola need all the help we can give them.

January 26:
Listening Is an Act of Love

. . . .

We don't always have to donate time and energy to other parts of the world. Sometimes help is needed much closer to home. Is a parent, sibling, spouse, or friend having a difficult time? Help lift their spirits by letting them experience that loving feeling. Invite them to coffee or to dinner, surprise them with a simple gift, or take them somewhere they like. Lean forward and listen closely. Just listen.

January 27:
Take a Walk on the Wild Side

You know you want to adopt a wild animal, don't you? Oceana's Adopt an Animal program allows you to be-friend (from a distance) a whale, manatee, puffin, sea turtle, or any number of beautiful sea creatures. Swim on over to oceana.org and bask in the richness dwelling within Earth's oceans.

January 28:
Warm and Fuzzies

Maybe you want to cozy up to your newly-adopted loved one—the World Wildlife Fund has a stuffed representa-tion of every imaginable animal, bird, fish or beyond. For a mere $55 donation on wildlife.org, you get an adop-tion certificate, a gift bag, and the long-distance love of a beastie! You can also get a photo of your new baby to show off to the relatives at holidays (what grandparent could resist a three-toed sloth, smiley orca, or scaly ant-eater in the family, really?).

January 29:
Wild in the Streets

. . . .

I live in a nice town adjacent to Berkeley, California, that is very urban, but I have a big ol' backyard, which I *love*—it is the reason I live here. I have raccoons, a family of squirrels, and a pair of deer who seem to love the yard as much as I do. One of the older trees bears a huge amount of apples every fall, much more than my boyfriend and I can cook or eat, not to mention our friends, coworkers, and deer and squirrels. So we bag up the extra apples and take them to a place where deer congregate at the edge of the woods a few blocks away. Every time I deliver a new bag, I see lots of deer tracks, showing that my four-legged forest friends enjoyed their apple a day. So before you just compost the excess bounty of your garden or fruit trees, take a look around and see who else might appreciate a neighborly gesture.

January 30:
200 Squares a Day

. . . .

Do you know how much an elephant needs to eat per day? At least 200 pounds of chow! Spring for $30 and you can feed a retired elephant all day long. Many of the denizens of the Elephant Sanctuary in Tennessee are former showgirls who left the three-ring circus behind them. Check out elephants.com for more details.

January 31:
Friends Are Not Just for Facebook

My newer pals are always kind of amazed that I have such a large group of friends, especially from back home in West Virginia. I attribute that to a few things: many of us come from Irish and Scottish stock, so we tend to be a wee bit clannish. We also check in on each other and get together quite regularly. There are the occasional squabbles but when trouble comes knocking, we have each other's backs all the way. It is a beautiful thing. When somebody moves, we are there to pack and tape boxes. When somebody is sick, we are there with homemade soup and a listening ear. To me, friendship is one of the most important things in the world and it is not just a phenomenon that takes place on social media.

chapter two

February

Love Is All Around

Love is the key to the solution of the problems of the world.

—DR. MARTIN LUTHER KING, JR.

February 1:
Help Girls Score!

Today is National Girls and Women in Sports Day. Started in 1987, it brings attention to the positive influence that sports participation has and to how it advances equality. The Women's Sports Foundation encourages moms to get more involved with their daughters' sports. Their website, womenssportsfoundation.org, gives lots of advice on how to get involved, prevent discrimination, and increase participation, along with information on coaching issues, clinics, funding, and more. Sports can be a huge help with young girls' self-confidence, skill, determination, and inner success, all of which can carry through into their later years. If you succeed in sports, you lead in life.

February 2:
Sharing Your Strength

When I worked on the Random Acts of Kindness project, we looked around for places to donate profits from the books and Share Our Strength came highly recommended. It remains an organization I deem to be a real good in the world. Did you know one in five children live in a home that struggles to put food on the table? Join SOS's campaign nokidhungry.org so we can take care of those who need it most.

February 3:
Helping Those Who Want to Help Themselves

We all remember the Biblical parable about teaching a man to fish so he can provide for himself and his family. Two thousand years later, we can do exactly this. My dad taught me how to fish in a pond back home on the farm in West Virginia. Even as a seven-year-old, I noticed that we not only got a couple day's worth of yummy trout for our efforts but my papa, a former Marine with many battle scars, seemed to relax after an afternoon at the pond. You can gift a $49 fishing kit in a loved one's name or set up a recurring monthly donation at Action Against

Hunger (ActionAgainstHunger.org), which feeds over 7 million people each year. Go fish!

February 4:
We All Have a Story

My dad loved to tell stories of being in World War II and he did have many dramatic tales of saving lives. He even delivered a Japanese POW's letter to his parents in Tokyo, a major act of kindness that involved a great deal of risk. I really wish I had recorded them, but I still carry dad's stories and share them in his honor. Our elders, in particular, have much to share and life lessons we could all learn from. The Library of Congress is gathering these by sending out volunteers to video record in the Veteran's History Project (loc.gov.vets). To me, one of the most special aspects of this oral history project is that it not only includes the Greatest Generation, but also features young people coming back from Iraq and Afghanistan, whose stories are equally precious. I think we are learning that every generation has true greatness.

February 5:
Thank-You Power

Upon learning about the Veteran's History Project, I was reminded that our servicemen and -women are doing just that: *service*. And they should be thanked for it. Many of these noble souls are very far away on active duty and receive little mail to their camp or barrack. Take a few moments to acknowledge their contribution and offer a friendly hello from back home in the USA. You can learn all about Operation Write Home at operationwritehome. gov. I have heard of great pen pal relationships that result from this gesture of gratitude.

February 6:
360 Degrees of Giving

My favorite kinds of gifts are the ones who keep on giving. The FEED Project has many cool options that are made in America and crafted with love and pride. A beautifully carved wooden cutting board for your best friend's birthday from FeedProjects.com will not only impress them but help feed the hungry. I love their FEED bags, which are a handy way to ditch the plastic and the paper, too.

February 7:
The Gift of Yourself

When I lived in the Lower Haight neighborhood of San Francisco, I drove for a food bank for AIDS patients in my rusted-out little car I had brought with me all the way from West Virginia. I had arrived in the mid-eighties, which we may all remember as the height of the AIDS crisis. One early morning, I was walking to the Church Street MUNI station and there was the food bank, with giant pink letters announcing itself as a place to lend a hand for the AIDS crisis. I went in and within two minutes had a shift and assignments for the week. Everyone in there seemed extremely cool to me. They were not grim at all, but seemed to have a mission of importance. It seemed such a small way to help during that scary time. I learned that regardless of what you can give, large or small, it is important to give of yourself. And it all does add up!

Feeding America is the largest hunger relief organization the United States and they need you. Please visit feedingamerica.org to find your local food bank or hunger organization. Get involved—you'll make a difference and you'll make friends along the way. I sure did, and they remain my friends to this day.

February 8:
Think with Your Heart

Shortly after retirement, Leon Delong, a very thoughtful Seattleite, wanted to utilize his new free time and he decided to do something meaningful. When he heard that city office towers were routinely throwing away half-used rolls of toilet paper, he started gathering them and delivering them to a local food bank, where they were given to the homeless and those in financial need. Over the last 15 years, the 76-year-old delivered over one million rolls of toilet paper. "I'm amazed how much this mattered to people," Delong said. "To me it was just a nice thing to do. Now, it's my claim to fame." What is your claim to fame?

February 9:
National Stop Bullying Day

Over three million students are victims of bullying each year. If you see someone being put down or harassed, stand up for them, or call the authorities if it's getting violent. Read more on how to help at dosomething.org. Stand up!

February 10:
It Is Getting Better

Join the 594,740 people who have taken the It Gets Better Pledge.

Have you taken the Pledge? Everyone deserves to be respected for who they are. I pledge to spread this message to my friends, family, and neighbors. I'll speak up against hate and intolerance whenever I see it, at school and at work. I'll provide hope for lesbian, gay, bisexual, transgender, and other bullied teens by letting them know that it gets better. Sign on up at itgetsbetter.org to support LGBTQ children and help teens live a bully-free life!

February 11:
Conscious Kindness

When I lived in the Panhandle District, I would occasionally wonder to myself from whence the name came. It is actually a skinny strip of land at the end of San Francisco's spectacular Golden Gate Park, like a handle on a skillet or big pan. But with so many down and out, there is a good bit of panhandling. In fact, it sometimes seems overwhelming, especially when, on any given day, I might be asked for money over a dozen times. I noticed that after 9/11, it became especially grim, as there was a scary economic downturn that accompanied all the other chaos. So I developed a system of my own: I always keep change in the little pocket of my driver's side door handle. And I prioritize giving to moms with kids, children, and amputees—anyone who really seems in need of help now. When I've been driving an author around on tour or out-of-town visitors, they have been startled when I mutter, "Oh, an amputee; let me see what I have on me." I explain my seeming rudeness by explaining that this is my personalized system for giving to panhandlers, and that I was almost an amputee. A few years back, I was hit and run by a drunk driver, which terribly injured my leg. My doctor suggested amputating—but I managed to talk him out of that idea. I had to learn to walk again. It took a looong time and caused a lot of pain. So I always think, "That could have been me!" and I want to help. Many a vet who served their country came back without a limb. This really is the least I can do and wanting to do more is one of the reasons behind this book.

February 12:
A Red Nose Can Change a Life

Whether they're juggling many balls at once, riding a unicycle or walking on very tall stilts, youth get a chance to shine on stage with the Prescott Circus Theater in Oakland, California. This youth development non-profit provides skill mastery, physical activity, and positive relationships with peers and adults. Their website, prescottcircus.org, goes on to say "the basic principles to succeed in circus (and in life) are: hard work, teamwork, practice, believe in yourself, and never give up." Donate to the Prescott Circus and you'll be sure to bring many more smiles to the world.

February 13:
Practice Random Acts of Kindness
(and Deliberate Ones, Too)

Random Acts of Kindness Day is always the week of Valentine's Day. I love to hear how this meaningful movement has touched others' lives. Artist and author Peg Conley shares her thoughts:

You've seen those bumper stickers, the ones encouraging you to commit "random acts of kindness?" What they can't tell you in that little space is how performing those acts can be a way of transforming yourself. When you begin to focus on extending kindness toward others, you'll feel more kindness coming toward you. Not only will you make someone else's day better, you'll be surprised at how well yours improves. It's rather like the "Secret Santa" gift exchange that many offices and families adopt during the weeks leading up to Christmas. There is delight when you do something for another while keeping your identity a secret. When you watch a person receiving a surprise gift, you see their face change, the eyes open wide with delight, a smile bursting into a grin, and laughter erupting. They appear to feel sheer joy at the unexpected. The old adage is true: "It is in giving that we receive." The other part of the quote, which is by a San Francisco writer named Anne Herbert, is often left out: "and (practice) senseless acts of beauty." I received a text the other day from a friend who had taken a picture with her phone of a sidewalk outside the coffee shop where she works in San Francisco. Someone had written "It's a beautiful day" with colored chalk on the sidewalk and adorned it with butterflies and hearts. That, to me, is a senseless act of beauty. Think how many people

walked on the sidewalk that day and smiled at the child-
ish scrawl reminding them of the beautiful day.

The Hebrew word mitzvah *means a good deed or an*
act of kindness. Judaism teaches that the world is built
on kindness. I recall what my Bubbe, a dear friend in
Salt Lake City who was my son's first caregiver, used
to tell me about the importance of doing mitzvahs. She
believes in the power of doing something good for an-
other person but not telling them about it. She is a per-
fect example of someone who practices random acts of
kindness, and also one who sees and acknowledges the
beauty in everyone she meets. I always feel better just
by being in her presence. Entire campaigns focused on
practicing random acts of kindness have sprouted up.
This, along with "having an attitude of gratitude," en-
riches my days in many ways. There are myriad ways
you can practice random acts of kindness. Don't forget
to include yourself when you are doing them!

February 14:
Valentine's Day

It's that sometimes-anticipated-by-couples-yet-often-dreaded-by-singles day of the year! In the spirit of Valentine's Day, send an anonymous letter or bouquet of flowers to someone special to you—your mom, your recently-divorced best friend. This deliberate act of kindness will last long after the 14th as the memory lingers on.

PS: A really nice thing to do the night before Valentine's Day is to offer to watch a friend or neighbor's children so they can run errands or spend time with their significant other.

February 15:
I Just Called to Say I Love You

Call your parents (or whoever raised you) and thank them for everything they did for you!

February 16:
Power for the Planet

Turn off your computer at night instead of leaving it on or in sleep mode, since this wastes energy. By doing so, you can save an average of 40 watt-hours per day, which adds up to four cents a day, or $14 per year (50waystohelp.com). In addition, the life of your computer will also be extended, as the amount of available time for virus contamination will be greatly reduced. This act of conservation is a great idea you should share with your office-mates.

February 17:
Be a Good Citizen

Rich Chin's family lived in New York City, pretty far away from any large expanse of wilderness, but that didn't get in his way. Rich shares his experience that first made him see how he could be a good in the world:

The Outward Bound Youth at Risk Program really helped many troubled teens get back on the "good citizen" road. I was one of those Outward Bound instructors that volunteered to teach in this life-changing experiment for inner city kids in the late seventies and eighties. It changed my life as much as it did those kids. I saw firsthand that if so-called "bad kids" were given a chance to learn how to respect others as well as themselves, they could contribute very positively and be part of our bright future.

Kurt Hahn founded Outward Bound (OutwardBound. org) on this assumption: "In genuine service to the benefit of others, one best expresses on a day-to-day basis his reverence for life itself."

February 18:
Planet-Positive and Paperless

Try paying bills online. By some estimates, if all households in the US paid their bills online and received electronic statements instead of paper, we'd save 18.5 million trees every year, 2.2 billion tons of carbon dioxide and other greenhouse gases, and 1.7 billion pounds of solid waste (50waystohelp.com).

February 19:
Be Ripsniptious!

Author Art Plotnik helped revive this word in his book *Better Than Great: A Plenitudinous Compendium of Wallopingly Fresh Superlatives.* Simply put, "ripsniptious" (*rip-snip-shuss*) can be used to express something or someone that is wonderful and highly spirited. Today, you will be ripsniptious and notice all of the other ripsniptious things around you. Let this be your word of the day and let it embody you—and introduce others to ripsniptiousness of the word ripsniptious! It's fun to say, isn't it? It's even better to be it. It is also a wonderful compliment and I think you are pretty darn ripsniptious for reading this book!

February 20:
Fur-Free and Fabulous

Don't buy fur, ivory, or other products derived from endangered animals. By purchasing these things, you are personally contributing to the extinction of an entire species without realizing it. And we *know* you don't want to do that. Fake fur is lots more fun. If you want to know specifics about poaching or endangered species, go to worldwildlifefund.org.

February 21:
Mindfulness at Mealtime

Eat like a Beatle! Sir Paul McCartney and many other celebrities support Meat Free Mondays. Check it out at meatlessmonday.com. The Belgian city of Ghent has instituted a Meat Free Thursday. Choose a day of the week to eat vegetarian or vegan and try to stick to this one-day diet each week. This global movement is saving water and preventing deforestation, not to mention its enormous health benefits!

February 22:
Throwing Shade: Trees Are Good for Us

Encourage community management of forests. If there are common property lands nearby you that are degraded, work with local communities and environmental NGOs to establish sustainable community forestry that benefits everyone. Get involved at treesforthefuture.org and meet your fellow tree huggers!

February 23:
Help Those Who Help Themselves

Empower an entrepreneur with a loan through Kiva. You can give as little as $25 to small business owners in developing countries to help eliminate poverty. Throughout the life of the loan, you will receive updates on the progress of the project and will be repaid by the borrower with Kiva Credit—which you can then use to fund another project. Through kiva.org, I have bought some really lovely pillows, baskets, and bangle bracelets made in India by creative, hard-working women.

February 24:
The 411

Your old cell phone is taking up space in your drawer when it could be helping a victim of domestic violence. Donate it to shelteralliance.net to keep your phone out of the landfill and know you are helping families in need.

February 25:
Detox Your Diet

Buy grass-fed, hormone-free, organic, and free-range meat, dairy, and eggs. Many grocery stores now have organic sections with produce that doesn't contain chemical fertilizers, pesticides, or herbicides. These choices are better for you and the earth because no chemicals go into the soil or water. These items cost a little more but for the sake of your health—and taste buds!—it's worth the price. Human-made pesticides and fertilizers require energy and resources to be manufactured and distributed; they also pollute air, soil, and water, and have been shown to be carcinogenic (cancer-causing) in many cases. Vegetables that are grown organically require less fossil-fuel energy to be grown, pollute less, and are far less likely to cause any health issues. Prevention Magazine (prevention.com) offers lots of good information about food safety and what to avoid. Healthier is also happier!

February 26:
Give Life

Donate blood. One donation can help up to four people. If that's not inspiring enough, every three seconds, someone needs a blood transfusion due to various injuries, illnesses, or conditions. Donating is completely free and completely safe at bloodcenters.org. Go to the American Red Cross website (redcrossblood.org/make-donation) to find a location near you. And did you know you get cookies and juice after your donation?

February 27:
Live Your Values

. . . .

When we are on track, living close to the things we deem important—the things we value—we feel happier. This isn't flash happiness, it isn't the kind that lasts for a few minutes when we get a new toy, or enjoy a concert. This is the kind that lingers in the background of our lives. The kind that even in moments of sadness or frustration, never completely disappears, because if we are living a values based-life we are also living with meaning and purpose.

—POLLY CAMPBELL

February 28:
Love Notes

. . . .

Leave encouraging, inspiring, or funny notes or quotes in a library book or other random places (without littering or defiling public property). A simple note stapled to a bulletin board, taped to a column, or written in chalk on the sidewalk may influence in wonderful ways—you'll be like a secret agent who brings happiness to others. This website has fun examples that might give you some ideas: artofgettingstarted.com.

Chapter three

March

Inspiration into Action

The only way to have a friend is to be one.

—RALPH WALDO EMERSON

March 1:
National Solo Vacation Day
. . . .

Go on vacation by yourself. Pick a town, state, or country that you have always wanted to go to and go there, alone! Think about it: you can make your own schedule, wake up when you want, stay out, stay in, and eat what you feel like. This is your chance at making a memory that will last you a lifetime and add to the story of your life.

March 2:
Let's Not Contribute to the
Great Pacific Garbage Patch
. . . .

I don't know about you, but photos of the big patch of plastic and garbage floating in the ocean scares me more than almost anything else. Nearly 90% of plastic bottles are not recycled, instead taking thousands of years to decompose. If you are used to toting around your green tea, juice, or iced coffee in plastic, get a cool-looking thermos instead. This is a great choice for the environment, your wallet, and possibly your health. You can guzzle as much as you want and still be green.

March 3:
Save the Rainforest

Tropical rainforests take in vast quantities of carbon dioxide (a poisonous gas which mammals exhale) and through the process of photosynthesis, convert it into clean, breathable air. In fact, the tropical rainforests are the single greatest terrestrial source of air that we breathe.

What's truly amazing, however, is that while the tropical rainforests cover just two percent of the Earth's land surface, they are home to two-thirds of all the living species on the planet. Additionally, nearly half the medicinal compounds we use every day come from plants endemic to the tropical rainforest. If a cure for cancer or the common cold is to be found, it'll almost certainly come from the tropical rainforests.

Tragically, the tropical rainforests are being destroyed at an alarming rate. According to Rainforest Action Network, more than an acre-and-a-half is lost every second of every day. That's an area more than twice the size of Florida that goes up in smoke every year!

According to savetherainforest.org, "If present rates of destruction continue, half our remaining rainforests will be gone by the year 2025, and by 2060 there will be no rainforests remaining."

March 4:
Please, Mr. Postman

Look into a pen pal. Writing to someone in a foreign land—whether it be a soldier, fellow student, or long-lost relative—can really help you gain perspective and will do the same for the person you are writing to. Check out this website for more details on how to find a pen pal: penpalworld.com. Letter writing is more meaningful than an email or text—this beautifully old-fashioned tradition will bring lasting enjoyment to you and your pal.

March 5:
The Language of Kindness

Learn a new language. Or become more fluent in your less dominant language if you are already multilingual. The more people you can communicate with, the more you'll make yourself available for work opportunities. Learning other languages will also open you up to new people and cultures. A friend of mine recently took a volunteer vacation where he taught English to orphans and abandoned children in Liberia. He said he enjoyed every minute and wants to do this every year, as he loved working with the kids. As he told me this story, his smile was at least a mile wide!

March 6:
Don't Be Judgmental; Be Kind Just Because You Can

"Contagious Optimist" Colleen Georges taught me this: It's easy to judge others for their actions and take for granted those we love or meet in chance encounters. We sometimes get so caught up in our busy-ness that we forget others are busy too, they have rough days just like us, and they benefit from our kindnesses just as we do theirs. Go out of your way to smile at strangers, say good morning, say thank you, give a compliment, and listen attentively to someone who needs your ear. Do it because you can, because it feels great, because it makes someone else feel good. Don't worry about a subsequent thank you; let a thank you be a beautiful perk, rather than an expectation.

March 7:
Share the Positive

When you read an online article that you found helpful, moving, or enlightening, take a moment to leave a positive comment on the bottom of the page. Acknowledge the writer for their style or content, or even add some additional information that you have about the topic. The writer—and other readers—may appreciate what you have to say. If it inspires you, share it, too. I started subscribing to lifehack.org and every morning, I come in to read some truly excellent and uplifting ideas in my inbox. I share the very best ones and have heard from Facebook friends and fellow Tweeps that they love 'em. So as the old saying goes, accentuate the positive!

March 8:
Lessen the Landfill in Your Daily Decisions

Diaper with a conscience. By the time a child is potty trained, a parent will have changed between 5,000 and 8,000 diapers, adding up to approximately 3.5 million tons of waste in US landfills each year. Whether you use cloth or a more environmentally friendly disposable alternative, you're making a choice that has a gentler impact on our planet.

March 9:
Stop World Hunger with Ten Grains of Rice a Day

Save a few dollars each month and donate it to a different charity. One great option for your donation is through freerice.com. For each correct answer in their online quizzes, they donate ten grains of rice to the World Food Program to help end world hunger. Think about how much rice will be donated if even half of the population did this!

March 10:
Make Amends

. . . .

It's never too late to say you're sorry. Apologize to someone you wronged in the past, especially if you stopped communicating because of the issue. By admitting fault and letting them know how sorry you are to have hurt them, you are taking responsibility for your actions and proving that you care enough for them to make things right. However bad you felt over the problem, you will feel five times better after making peace.

March 11:
Cloth Napkins Are Nicer Anyway

. . . .

On average, an American uses around six napkins each day—2,200 a year! If every American used even one less napkin per day, more than one billion pounds of napkins could be saved from landfills each year.

March 12:
Buddy Up

. . . .

Teach your children, or the children in your family, about the buddy system. According to the Amber Alert website, a child goes missing every 40 seconds in the United States and more than 700,000 children go missing annually. In order to ensure the safety of your children, teach them to hold your hand when out in public; not to talk to or go off with strangers; remember their phone number and address; and to yell "FIRE!" rather than "HELP!" if someone is trying to hurt or take them—this will gain more people's attention. Every child we save will make for a better future.

March 13:
Be a Good Samaritan

. . . .

Did you know this is National Samaritan Involvement Day? Now you do, and I have no doubt you can immediately be helpful to someone, somewhere. Doing a favor for someone without expecting something in return is the epitome of kindness and will earn you some karma points down the line (though you shouldn't do this with the expectation of any!). Sometimes helping others is the best way to help yourself. Anytime one of my friends is singing the blues, I will say, "Let's go serve some beans down at Glide Memorial! You'll stop feeling sorry for yourself in the first 60 seconds."

March 14:
Use Your Words

I read all the time as a child, and by that I mean every minute I wasn't at school, doing chores or homework, or sleeping, I had the cover of a book open. I developed a love of language that has lasted me a lifetime. I notice that it brings joy to others when they hear an interesting or pretty word. So try flipping through a dictionary every day and pick a word. Use this word at least once in the same day. This will help expand your vocabulary and communicate better with others. If you have a smartphone, download a free word-of-the-day app instead of using a dictionary. Help feed a child by adding a definition to the Online Community Dictionary on definition-of.com.

March 15:
A Book Can Change Your Life

Give someone a copy of a book that has helped or influenced you—it may have a similar effect on them. I actually keep a stock of books that I love on hand to do just that and have recently gifted quite a few copies of *The Power of Habit* by Charles Duhigg. Give it a read.

March 16:
The Little Things Count

Do little things for others, like holding the door open and letting someone go before you, or allowing the person with only one item go ahead of you at the grocery store. I think due to our over-busyness nowadays, so many people rush through life and don't consider the feelings of others. A simple gesture can be a good reminder for us all, myself included. Take your time, look around you, and ask yourself, how can I help someone today? In the end, you are also helping yourself just as much.

March 17:
Be a Visionary

Did you know your old specs can have a second act? Old prescription eyeglasses can be donated to a LensCrafters store. Every LensCrafters business supports OneSight, which provides glasses to millions of people around the globe. Learn more at lenscrafters.com/onesight.

March 18:
Be a Good in Your Hood

Pick up and recycle or compost loose garbage as you walk. Sidewalks are meant for safe walking, not weaving through someone else's abandoned bottles and crumpled up take-out bags. Take pride in the area you live and help contribute to keeping it clean and safe. One person helping can inspire many others to do the same. I vowed to do this 15 years ago when living in the Lower Haight in San Francisco. By the end of each week, I usually had a big bag to take to the HANC Recycling Center. In the last couple of years, I have gotten some puzzled glances and even laughter when I am dressed up for a meeting while walking down the street and picking up garbage, empty bottles, and what-have-you. I will occasionally say, "This

is my service to the earth. Recycling is my religion."
And it is. I have the planet's back!

March 19:
Treat People Well

Bring homemade goodies to work. For many of us, we work five days a week with the same people in the same office for the same amount of hours. What could be more uplifting than arriving at work to the sight and smell of baked goods or snacks? Make something that most people would enjoy, such as chocolate chip cookies or banana bread. The work environment will become more warm and inviting, and making others feel good is one of the true pleasures in life.

March 20:
The Best Kind of Social Networking

Help the elderly with their devices. Many senior citizens aren't tech-savvy, but given that we live in a technologically advancing society, learning how to use a computer or the Internet can be very helpful. Volunteer your assistance to a senior who has a cell phone or computer and needs help using it. Be email buddies with your new friends, too!

March 21:
Use Your Common Cents

Lend a helping hand. Next time the person in front of you in line at the cash register is short a few cents, give them the amount they need.

March 22:
Welcome to the World!

Assemble a baby care kit to help young mothers in need with newborns. Visit the Church World Service website for information on what to pack and where to send the shipment at cwsglobal.org/get-involved/cws-kits/baby-care-kits.html.

March 23:
The Healing Power of Touch

Be a baby cuddler. According to this excellent guide for volunteers at volunteerguide.org/hours/service-projects/baby-cuddlers, "Baby cuddlers are needed in orphanages, neonatal hospital units, group homes, nurseries, and wherever else there are babies and young children who may not have adequate human contact early in life to begin developing social interaction skills." What could be better than helping a baby survive and thrive?

March 24:
Power Down

Switch off the lights when you leave a room, don't leave the faucet running if you're not actively using it, use energy-saving light bulbs, opt for blankets over turning on the heater and choose portable fans over air conditioning... All of these will lower your utility bills and help preserve the planet. It just makes *cents* (get it?). If every household in the United States replaced one regular light bulb with one of those new compact fluorescent bulbs, the pollution reduction would be equivalent to removing one million cars from the road.

March 25:
Reimagine and Reuse Every Chance You Get

In addition to recycling, you should also strive to reuse. When wrapping presents, use old maps or even newspaper—or open up a paper grocery bag, flip it over, and have your kids customize the paper with their artwork. You can also keep and reuse gift bags and tissue paper you were once given. This will save you money on buying gift-wrap while helping the environment save a few more trees.

March 26:
Make Up Your Own Holiday

Invent a special holiday to celebrate someone you love—be it your spouse, your dog, or your closest friend. On this day, make them a special dinner, take them out, and write them a letter saying how you feel about them. You can even create a fun holiday to share with your family so everyone can participate.

March 27:
Share Your Hair

Do you have long hair, or don't mind growing it out for a good cause? Donate to Locks of Love, a group truly contributing to the good of others. Visit their website at locksoflove.org for more information. I recently read of a five-year-old girl who gave her hair to a fellow kindergartner going through chemo. With kids like her in the world, our future is bright!

March 28:
I Love Big Bags and I Cannot Lie

Bring reusable shopping bags when heading to the store. Whether you are grocery shopping or heading out with friends to splurge on clothes, take your own bags with you. Many stores have totes and reusable bags for a few dollars by the checkout lines that are more durable, hold more objects, and last much longer than those flimsy paper and non-biodegradable plastic bags. Reusable shopping bags help the environment by using less plastic and cutting down fewer trees.

March 29:
Earth Hour Day

Participate in Earth Hour today, beginning at 8:30 pm in the United States, and turn off all of the lights in your home for one hour. Earth Hour (earthhour.org) unites millions of people around the world and gives them the hope that together we can make a difference. Take this hour to sit with your significant other or invite some pals over for a candlelit evening of togetherness. Just be. Together.

March 30:
Say My Name

When meeting new people, make an effort to remember their name so that when you address them, it's more personal, respectful, and will make a good impression on them. Everyone is important. When you see them the next time, greet them by name. So simple, so nice.

March 31:
Go Forth and See the World

· · · · · · · · · · · ·

I am reminded by the peripatetic Phil Cousineau that travel is a very important tool for lasting happiness and creating memories to savor over a lifetime. Phil, author of essential guides to making travel meaningful *The Art of Pilgrimage* and *The Book of Roads*, says it is important to "go out of your way," and meet people that are native to the place you're visiting. He also reminds us to give gifts, simple tokens from your homeland, and gestures of goodwill that will be returned a thousandfold.

Over 2,000 years ago, the sage Lao Tzu remarked, "The longest journey starts with a single step." Phil says to use "the eyes of the heart" when traveling to learn something about yourself and the wide world around you. Here are some of Phil's recommended practices for making travel meaningful:

Imagine your first memorable journey. What images rise up in your soul? They may be of a childhood visit to the family gravesite, the lecture your uncle gave at a famous battlefield, or the hand-in-hand trip with your mother to a religious site. What feelings are evoked by your enshrined travel memories? Do they have any connection with your life today? Have you ever made a vow to go someplace that is sacred to you, your family, your group? Have you ever imagined yourself in a place that stirred your soul like the song of doves at dawn? If not you, then who? If not now, when? If not here, where? Paris? Benares? Memphis?—Uncover what you long for and you will discover who you are.

chapter four

April

We Live on a Beautiful Planet

Align your life with your values and your love.

—JOHN ROBBINS

April 1:
No Foolin'

. . . .

I don't know the history of April Fool's Day trickster antics but they always make me cringe. I suggest a "reverse prank" instead, where you do something really nice. I heard through the Random Acts of Kindness network about a good deeder buying lottery tickets, adding a sweet little note, and placing them onto a car door where they could not be missed. Can you imagine if you were the recipient of this delightful act and won the big Scratch Off for a cool million or so?

Have fun and bring some joy into this early spring day. It may be April Fool's Day but don't fool yourself! Today is about laughter rather than pulling pranks on others. Tell your coworkers a joke you enjoy; find a way to make someone who looks unhappy put a smile on their face.

April 2:
No Strings Attached

Write down the things that someone has given you, no strings attached, for which you are grateful. It can be an old sofa, some sound advice, or a lift to the airport. Now list ten things that you would like to give someone yourself, and see how many of those things you can cross off in a week.

Examples:

- Drive a friend to the airport.
- Carry groceries for an elder to their car.
- Babysit for a relative.
- Buy a friend a cup of coffee.
- Volunteer at a soup kitchen.

April 3:
Make Beautiful Music

If you're a musician living in New York City, Philadelphia, Washington, DC, Nashville, or Miami, you can volunteer through the nonprofit Musicians on Call (musiciansoncall.org) to deliver live, in-room performances to patients undergoing treatment or unable to leave their beds. Add a dose of joy to a healthcare facility by bringing the healing power of music to people who need it.

April 4:
Have a Mission and Live By It

Tucker Hiatt, one of the Bay Area's most beloved teachers, has been running Wonderfest—a nonprofit science education program—with his own and donated funds since 1997 (Wonderfest.org). The mission is based on the insight, inspired by Voltaire, that "societies will continue to make mistakes as long as they continue to misunderstand how the world works. When people comprehend nature and each other, through science, they make smarter decisions about virtually everything: personal and social relationships (psychology), our environment (biology and chemistry), and technology (physics)." Wonderfest promotes the scientific outlook so that mistakes—even atrocities—are gradually relegated to history. Since retiring from teaching, Tucker has devoted himself full time to bringing science to the public in non-school settings. Whenever I'm at an event with him I meet former students of his who have become physicists, engineers, professors—and still talk about how influential he was to them. Now his mission is to expose those of us who didn't get to have him as a teacher (my words, not his!) to that same sense of inspiration.

Some cool things Tucker and his organization have accomplished:

- Wonderfest has presented hundreds of free (or nearly free) science events for the general public—young and old.
- Wonderfest ran a high school team science competition that gave students $70,000 in prizes and scholarships.
- Wonderfest has rewarded local, public-spirited scientists with $45,000 with its Sagan Prize.

April 5:
Be a Fixer-Upper (Plus Weeding Is Good Therapy)

Assist seniors near you with tasks like raking, shovel-ing, or doing minor home repairs through Volunteers of America's Safety of Seniors Handyman Program (voa. org). I pull my 98-year-old neighbor's weeds and it is good exercise for me, it beautifies the neighborhood, and she appreciates the weekly attention she and her yard enjoy!

April 6:
Free Hugs for All!

Be an indiscriminate hugger. When I first moved to Cali-fornia, I was a bit taken aback by all the hugging. Now, I love it. Be a hugger. A hug is a mutual act of love and affection that induces feelings of comfort, contentment, and security. Hugs are one of the most beautifully human things we can do.

April 7:
Save Seeds

My Aunt Ruth in Flat Rock, West Virginia raised me to save seeds. A child of the Great Depression, my Aunt Ruth was teaching me the virtue of thrift when she showed me how to harvest, dry, and save seeds from veggies and flowers. Thrift was an important survival skill for that time and I see it as a forgotten virtue whose time has arrived once again. I remember being very impatient about how long it took for spring to come so I could sow the marigolds, alyssum, and four o' clocks that I had collected.

April 8:
And Don't Forget the Senseless Acts of Beauty!

Ann Herbert, the poet artist who inspired Random Acts of Kindness, also implored us to add prettiness to the world. There are so many ways to do this: plant flowers, pick up trash, or paint a lovely mural for the entire neighborhood's pleasure.

What beauty can you bring to the world?

April 9:

Participate in the Gift Economy

Free markets are one of the ways that people have figured out how to cooperate when finances are uncertain. It is one of my absolute favorite examples of a gift economy, where people come together with items to give away or share. The Really Really Free Market (reallyreallyfree. org) is a great prototype. No money changes hands. Participants simply bring their offerings and display them communally.

People also bring their expertise and talents to share: lawyers, musicians, jugglers, gardeners, ecologists, hairdressers, tarot readers, and cookie bakers are all there enjoying this unique marketplace. It provides as much diversity as the market economy, and for free!

The Really Really Free Market website lists 34 regular free markets happening in states across the US and another ten or so worldwide in places like Perth, Australia. Your city could be the next.

April 10:
Calling All Cat Cuddlers

Yes, there is such a thing as ASPCA (American Society for the Prevention of Cruelty to Animals) Day. Consider rescuing an animal from a shelter, and if you can't do that, volunteer at your local animal shelter as a dog walker, cat cuddler, or whatever else they need. Most of my friends who adopt a pet are at least 200% happier thanks to their new family member.

April 11:
National Pet Day

If you have a pet, make sure you give them attention every day. Even if you can only afford to spend ten minutes with them, that time is enough to show them that you care and to make them feel loved. Pets need love as much as people do. The responsibility of caring for your pet's life includes dedicating time and affection toward them.

April 12:
Go Solar

Solar ovens are inexpensive and easy to use, and you'll cook for free every time you use one. Since it doesn't require electricity, fossil fuels, or propane, a solar oven is perfect for your emergency supply kit. They also pasteurize water for drinking. Check out solarovens.org to see the great work this nonprofit is doing with solar ovens in developing countries. Go solar and really worship the sun.

April 13:
Be a Freecycler

For me, the coolest of the online free resource sites is Freecycle (freecycle.org). The Freecycle Network initiative started in Tucson in 2003, when Deron Beal sent out the first email to 30 or so friends and local nonprofits letting them know about the items he had to give away. Freecycle now has 4,738 groups worldwide and an amazing 6,690,000 members. Just think about how many wonderful free treasures have changed hands and the sheer tonnage saved from landfill. Bravo, Mr. Beal!

Freecycle's mission is to save good stuff from the landfill, promote environmental sustainability, and imbue life with the spirit of generosity, creating stronger local communities in the process.

The steps to join a Freecycle group are straightforward. If there isn't a group in your area yet, you can start one. Once you have joined your local group, you can begin to post messages for what you want and what you have to offer. Freecycle is administered by volunteers and has the great advantage of not needing a physical location—Freecycle's easy-to-use listing website makes it nearly effortless to use. Some posts are for significant items such as computers, bicycles, televisions, stereos, and even cars. Offering your surplus and finding what you need for free are both gratifying experiences, and ultimately, they alleviate a lot of stress on our precious planet.

April 14:

Hold a Closet Swap Soiree

You can share your surplus clothing with friends and acquaintances by throwing a "naked lady party." This is a fun way to exchange clothes as well as other items. First, set a date, and invite a group of friends to your house (we do ladies only, but men could be included, too) and ask everybody to bring some clothes that they don't want anymore. Set up your living room as a shop, designating different areas for guests to deposit their items—dresses in one pile, sweaters in another, and so on. Be sure to make a bedroom available for those friends who are too shy to try on clothes in company. We usually drink wine and have some snacks, and we end up with bags of new-to-us clothing. Don't be bashful—things that you are heartily sick of will be starring in somebody else's wardrobe, and the surplus can be dispatched to the thrift store.

April 15:
Eat for the Environment

Cutting back on meat consumption is good for the environment, your health, and your wallet. Producing one pound of beef puts as much carbon dioxide into the environment as driving a typical car 70 miles! Read "Livestock's Long Shadow," the 2006 UN paper about the effects of the meat industry on the environment and human populations, at fao.org/docrep/010/a0701e/a0701e00.HTM.

April 16:
Support Farm-to-School Projects

By teaching kids exactly where their food comes from, they will grow up to make informed grocery choices and strengthen their local economies. Start a farm-to-school project in your school district; all the know-how is at farmtoschool.org.

April 17:
Extend an Invitation to Life's Rich Banquet

If you see a uniformed soldier or veteran in a restaurant, arrange to pay for their meal. Anonymously is perfect unless you want to thank them personally and "enlist" a new friend into your life!

April 18:
Roll Out the Welcome Wagon

Greet your new neighbors with a homemade housewarming gift. You'll make a new connection and help them feel more at home. Good neighbors can last a lifetime and bring a real sense of community on a daily basis.

April 19:
Be of Good Cheer

Open the doors for everyone—young, old, everyone in between—simply because it is a very, very, very nice thing to do.

April 20:
Pass on the Wisdom of Grandmothers
to Children Today

Rich, my beloved, was raised by his grandmother, whom he called "GM." She had been the wife of the head of their village and clan in Southern China until the Japanese Occupation, when war devastated the community at the great cost of many lives. She felt very *fook sing* (lucky) to have made it to America with her only son and they rebuilt their lives from scratch. She ran a Chinese laundry, which I have no doubt was the finest in all of Flushing, Queens. While working and taking care of her grandchildren, she told stories of the homeland, including the hardest times of having to eat insects during drought and war, famine, and pestilence. She relayed all this with no bitterness, only a sense of great good fortune in getting to live in the land of plenty in the US. Day by day, story-by-story, she instilled values of excellence—gratitude, hard work, keeping a positive attitude no matter what—in her children and grandchildren.

When Rich and his younger brother Jimmy went to public school in Queens, they made lots of friends in that melting pot metropolis, including a young African

American boy who was really tall for his age and came from a family that had a hard time putting enough food on the table. One day, he stopped by her house with Rich and Jimmy. It took GM about two seconds to assess the situation and she told them to bring him by every day. She always made extra for their new fast-growing buddy. Having faced severe hunger during the war, GM was not going to let anybody in her circle go hungry.

Every day, in ways large and small, she showed her family how to do the right thing—stand on the bus so others can sit, be polite even if others are rude and, above all, "Take care of your clan."

April 21:
Top of the Mornin'

One of our fabulous interns here at Viva Editions, Sara Wigglesworth, has a lovely way of saying "Good morning" upon arriving that ensures it will actually be a better day. I have to admit that greeting coworkers sometimes slips my mind, so it's helpful to be reminded of the power that a simple, well-intentioned, and sincere greeting can have. It is a wonderful way to start the day with elegance and ease.

April 22:
Celebrate Earth Day Every Day!

This is the day to acknowledge your connection to your home planet and all the nurturing nature, bounty, and beauty you receive from this big blue dot. April 22 is Earth Day, celebrated annually in over 184 countries to promote a healthy environment and a peaceful planet. Earth Day highlights our connection with nature, bringing awareness that each one of us is responsible for the destruction or abundance of our natural world...the only one we have. Earth Day makes us realize that each of us has a voice and every one of our actions matters; collectively great things happen.

Celebrate Earth Day by joining an organized group and help clear beaches and parks of cans, paper, plastic, bottles, and trash. Go with your family and friends, or go out alone. Look around in your neighborhood to see what needs to be done. Petition your local government for more trees, cleaner waterways, and an end to industrial pollution. Use earth-friendly chemicals. Recycle paper and cans, and compost green matter.

Log onto earthday.org or check your local press to find out what is happening in your area, how to organize your own event, or what commitment you could make in your own small way to help save our Earth...and then make every day Earth Day.

April 23:
Breathe Easier

Having plants around is great for where you live and where you work. Not only are they lovely to look at, they improve the air you breathe! The following air-purifying plants look great, produce oxygen, and can even absorb contaminants like formaldehyde and benzene (commonly off-gassed from furniture and mattresses). The best part? Nary an electrical cord, nor a battery in sight. Ahhhhh.

- Spider plant
- Peace lily
- Snake plant
- Elephant ear
- Weeping fig
- Rubber plant
- Bamboo palm

April 24:
Be a Pre-cycler

Try to recycle all the product packaging that an item comes in, from the cardboard box to the plastic sleeve. Buy fewer, but better-quality, products to ensure you won't end up with a makeup drawer filled with stuff that doesn't live up to its promises. And finally, check out companies like TerraCycle (terracycle.com) that offer recycling programs for things like mascara tubes and lotion bottles. I am very proud that on my business card, alongside my title of "Publisher," it also says "Office Composter" because I set up a full-scale recycling and zero waste program. Visitors dig it!

April 25:
Making the Most of a Rainy Day

Get a rain barrel:

- Install the rain barrel at least six feet from your house. Locating it near the area you'll be watering the most makes for convenient use later.
- Ensure that your rain barrel has an overflow at least as large as your inflow—for example, if you

have rigged it so that water is collected directly from your eaves' trough downspout, your over-flow valve should be as large as your downspout as well. This will allow your barrel to get rid of excess water as fast as it collects it, which might be necessary if you live in a city with crazy, unpredictable weather like my brother does.

● If you are using the rain barrel to water your garden, consider using a soaker hose. You can attach the hose to the rain barrel and then run it through your garden so that it covers the area you'd like. Now, every time you see a rain cloud, you'll get really excited!

April 26:
Planting Trees Is Good for All

In 1872, J. Sterling Morton founded Arbor Day, and that year over a million trees were planted in Nebraska. It's usually celebrated on the last Friday in April (some states choose different dates depending on their weather for best tree planting times). Probably now, more than ever, we need to honor Morton's big idea—trees hugely improve the quality of our lives. They provide shelter and food for our wildlife, clean the air, absorb carbon dioxide, and release oxygen. They mask noise, prevent soil erosion, and provide wood for fuel and buildings: all this plus the joy and wonder of such a majestic and wonderful plant.

Celebrate Arbor Day by logging onto arborday.org and finding out what you can do in your area. Save a tree by recycling paper. Plant a suitable tree in your garden or neighborhood and dedicate it to someone special.

April 27:
More Ways to Avoid Plastic

- Jars. So many jars. For salads, soups, sauces, juice, opened packages of things. Just jars. Lots of jars.
- Aluminum foil is a great stand-in for plastic wrap and can be easily recycled or saved for reuse.
- Wax paper is great for wrapping sandwiches. So are reusable sandwich pouches you can make or purchase. Many close with Velcro and are easy to launder or wipe clean.
- Reuse empty yogurt, sour cream, or cream cheese containers. You've already got them and you have to wash them before tossing them into the

recycling bin anyway, so you may as well use them again.

● Invest in reusable lunch containers like bento boxes or tiffins to avoid waste when sending off your little one (or yourself) with a bagged lunch.

April 28:
Just Say No to GMO

Buy organic heritage seedlings whenever you can. Most fruits and vegetables have an incredibly diverse range of varieties, but we typically only see one or two different kinds in the grocery store. By choosing to grow heritage plants we can preserve that diversity and give a big green thumbs down to monoculture.

April 29:
Water Is Life

Give up the bottled water. Please? Not only is it ridiculously overpriced and horrifically wasteful, but also it fails to offer any benefit over tap water. Many brands draw their water from a municipal supply—as in, the same water that comes out of your tap for free. Additionally, bottled water companies aren't held to the same stringent standards as public waterworks. And, adding final insult to injury, plastic bottles can often leach harmful chemicals into the water and then languish in landfills for thousands of years if not properly recycled. It's better for everyone involved if you carry a jar or reusable water bottle to fill up instead. Drinking from a Mason jar is the ultimate in chic, too!

April 30:
Ditch the High-Maintenance Front
Lawn and Plant Natives

As a Northern Californian experiencing a serious drought, I am thrilled to see more and more gardens being cultivated with plants that need *no* water. This method is called xeriscaping and it is gorgeous and has enormous variety. If you're tired of the constant mow/water/fertilize cycle of your lawn, consider getting rid of it altogether. It's not as bizarre as it sounds. Some water conservationists estimate that up to 40% of a household's water usage during the summer months is spent on outdoor watering, so ditching the lawn altogether can save you time and money, not to mention a precious resource. One eco-friendly option is to replace all that turf with plants indigenous to your region, which will require less water and look far prettier than any plain ol' square of green grass ever could. Start a xeriscaping movement on your street.

chapter five

May

Your Garden Will Grow You

A garden is a living symbol of optimism, proof that patience has its rewards and confirmation that tender loving care cultivates beauty.

—VERONICA HUNSUCKER

May 1:

Plant Flowers in Abandoned Lots

• • • • • • • • • • • • •

May Day was a sacred celebration of spring in ancient times and remains a special day for modern folk. I have attended several marvelous festivities complete with garlanded Maypoles; one held by Z Budapest is a treasured memory. I have my own tradition for this merry month, which is a really simple and easy way to celebrate spring: I plant flower seeds in neglected plots of land all around the Bay Area, particularly nasturtiums, which thrive on neglect and can bloom anywhere and under any circumstances. I could give a driving tour of San Francisco and the East Bay and show you the brightly colored patches that are the result of my Johnny Appleseed-style scattershot approach. You can even eat them! I always have a lot of nasturtiums growing in my garden and I collect the seeds once they have flowered in plastic baggies. I joke to my friends that I would like my legacy to be that I was "Fiesta Blenda," the name of a mix that yields a riot of color that can turn any former parking lot or weed patch into a pocket of red, yellow, and orange sunshine. I will add that some of my tenth-generation crop mutated into a lovely variegated leaf, which only adds to the glory.

This bit of freeganomics feeds my soul like almost nothing else. I would say it is a sensible act of beauty.

May 2:
True Love Does Not Require a Diamond

Precious gems and metals leave a horrific trail of pollution and human rights abuses. Not much more needs to be said about this one without getting into some seriously depressing territory, but we cannot discuss jewelry without acknowledging that many people pay a steep price in order to mine, produce, and export all those shiny little rocks we coyly call "a girl's best friend." There are so many ways to show your love and no suffering should be involved. Ever.

Seeds

May 3:
Unplug (and Recharge!)

Forego using technological devices today. Texting your friend, watching your favorite show, checking your email—all can wait until tomorrow! Turn off your devices and turn on your senses! Read a book, cook a meal, and enjoy the outdoors by taking a walk or tending to your garden. Technology distracts us from the real world, occupying our attention with game applications, chat rooms, social media websites, commercials, and so on. Want to know what's going on in the news? Read a newspaper. Be aware of the here and now by finding activities that don't require electricity or a battery. Make your own entertainment!

May 4:
National Lemonade Day

Instead of driving past yet another lemonade stand, help the kids out by pulling over and buying a cup on a hot day. The kids will feel a sense of accomplishment as more people follow your example. Model good behavior whenever you can and it will return to you in spades.

May 5:
Stories Are Not Just for Bedtime

Read a child a story. Introducing children to the world of books while they're young will help boost their imagination and intelligence (and will also strengthen your bond). Whether you are babysitting, reading to your own child, or volunteering at a library or hospital, this deed goes a long way.

May 6:
For Services Rendered

Send a letter to someone in local law enforcement, the Coast Guard, or serving overseas that gives thanks for their hard work and dedication to our country. It's simple and will be greatly appreciated. Go to LetsSayThanks. com for inspiration.

May 7:
List Your Life

Instead of writing up and crossing things off of a bucket list, create a "life list." Let your hopes, dreams, fears, and thoughts spill out of you and into this list. Next to each entry, write down how that emotion or fear makes you feel—does it hold you back or empower you? This task will put you on the road to self-discovery. Knowing who you are is important in order to have relationships with others. Know thyself.

May 8:
Moving and Grooving

Moving? Use clean sheets, pillowcases, and towels to pack breakable items like dishes and framed artwork. The soft material will help cushion your breakables, reducing or eliminating the need for bubble wrap. As an added bonus, linens and kitchen items are also usually among the first things you'll need to unpack at your new place, so using one to help pack the other means you'll find everything you need in one box. Clever, eh?

May 9:
Do the Thing You Think You Cannot Do

My friend Clare Cooley practices this courageous philosophy and now teaches others how to "Imagine a Day." Clare is probably the ultimate autodidact; she had to drop out of school pretty early to take care of family members. This has not stopped her from learning and doing anything she sets her mind to, from design, filmmaking, and painting to crafting, writing, and music. One of Clare's most spectacular gifts is her show-stopping skate dancing and there are many YouTube videos that strangers have taped and uploaded of her whirling and twirling. Clare, who chose to not allow economic difficulties and a lack of formal education prevent her from succeeding in life, has gone on to show her ceramics and naturalist paintings in museums and galleries around the country. She says, "Lack of imagination is the only limitation and fear creates self-doubt." In her teaching, she helps people get out of "fear mode" and unlock the power of imagination. You can see her beautiful artwork at clarecooley.com.

I urge you to Imagine a Day—pick something you always wanted to do, but were afraid to try. Painting, French cookery, playing piano, singing, learning a foreign language, yoga, rock-climbing, ballroom dancing, pottery, snorkeling—something that speaks to you on a profound level but scares you just a little. Find a class or barter with someone who is an expert to whom *you* can teach something, and dive right in.

May 10:
Mother Ocean Day

Look into volunteering to clean up your local beach. With pollution in our water and in the sand, help make these local hot spots safer for visitors to the beach and the environment! If you live in the San Francisco Bay Area, check out All One Ocean to see when you can help: alloneocean.org/community-meeting-beach-clean-up.

May 11:
Love Your Mother

Celebrate your mother today by making her feel special and loved by taking her out to lunch or a mani/pedi. For your friends who may have lost their mother, check in with them as this day may be difficult. Mother's Day is *all* about love, so spread it around far and wide.

May 12:
Ask "How Are You?" and Mean It!

Ask someone how their day is going and start a conversation. Sometimes people want to talk more than they let on and your interest will show them you care. One day, you'll get the chance to tell some kind-hearted person exactly how *you* are. Your answer to that question might not always be pretty, but it will feel wonderful to be heard.

May 13:
A Very Very Very Fine House

Volunteer to help build a house through Habitat for Humanity (habitat.org), a nonprofit organization that builds and repairs houses so that families have a safe and affordable place to live. Maybe you'll even get to meet former President Jimmy Carter and you can hammer up a front porch and discuss world peace together.

May 14:
Lit Love

Every child should learn to expand their mind through the wide world of literature. The fine folks at Books for Kids (booksforkids.org) have a love of reading and have helped disadvantaged families collect libraries at home. You can make that happen, one kid and one book at a time. Pick out some of your favorites that you loved as a child and get in on the fun.

May 15:
The Keys to Kindness

If you are like me, you can end up with so many old keys you end up looking like a janitor! Find out how you can unlock some goodness at keysforkindness.com. Donate your old keys to help fight Multiple Sclerosis.

May 16:
Games That Give

Even online gaming can be philanthropic—try out Games That Give, at gamesthatgive.net/play. This website donates approximately 70% of their advertising revenue to charitable causes. Everyone wins here.

May 17:
Making Sure She Has a Night to Remember

Did you know that many teen girls long to attend their high school prom but end up missing out on the tradition simply because a fancy dress is not in the family budget? Help these girls out by visiting www.glassslipperproject.org.

Donate your old prom dress and shoes to the delightful folks at the Glass Slipper Project, a nonprofit organization that gives free prom dresses, shoes, and accessories to high school juniors and seniors. Generosity can be very glamorous!

May 18:

A Laugh a Day Keeps the Doctor Away

As the legendary Charlie Chaplin said, "A day without laughter is a day wasted."

Laughter and good humor are infectious. Sharing a funny story or memory with others helps increase happiness and intimacy between friends, acquaintances, and loved ones. According to helpguide.org, laughter triggers happiness and can strengthen the immune system, boost energy, relieve physical and emotional pain, and battle the effects of stress. Today is a great day! Let yourself enjoy it.

May 19:

Let's Make It a Complaint-Free World

Go one day without complaining. Even better, go a week. If this is hard for you to accomplish, it's time to make some changes in your life. Think positively, live in the present, and appreciate where you are and who you are. Today is a gift, so accept and embrace it.

Author Mark Bowen wrote a fantastic book on this very topic that I turn to when I need a reminder, as we all do now and again. My copy came with a bracelet, a simple way to monitor how often you complain that helps you track your progress toward becoming "complaint-free." Put on the bracelet and every time you complain, switch it to the other wrist. The goal is to go 21 consecutive days without switching the bracelet. It is harder than you might think and I was a bit shocked at what a complainer I turned out to be. It was a really good exercise for me—I highly recommend it. I benefited enormously and I suspect those around me did, too!

May 20:
Penning the Positive

Write a message of positivity on a decorated postcard and send it in to postsecret.com. There, you can also view postcards that others have sent in. Affirmations, love notes, and written acts of kindness truly have the power to lift the human spirit.

May 21:
National Endangered Species Day

Did you know monarch butterflies are at risk of becoming extinct? Protect wildlife and endangered animals. Join a preservation group or animal sanctuary to help keep our habitats and animals safe. More than 800 animals have gone extinct over the last 500 or so years, according to the International Union for Conservation of Nature and Natural Resources' Red List—generally considered to be the most comprehensive of its kind. Our diversity is what makes Earth so special and we must do all we can do to preserve it.

May 22
Let Kids Be Kids

Finding out that handmade rugs are often made by mere children was so shocking to me—I couldn't imagine what those youngsters have to go through every day. The organization GoodWeave (goodweave.org) was started in 1994 to stop child labor in the rug industry. To help their efforts, check for a GoodWeave label on the rugs you purchase and donate to their One in a Million campaign. GoodWeave's work has reduced the numbers of children toiling in rug factories, and with your help, they can help end child labor in the world today.

May 23:
You Have the Power!

Anonymously grant a wish on someone's Amazon wish list. How simple is that? And how sweet is that?

May 24:
Share Your Toys

Leave small, handmade toys for people to find. The Toy Society spreads love by doing this good deed. Visit thetoysociety.blogspot.com for more information and insipiration. You can post your toy drop on the website and view the drops that others have made. Feel free to share a picture and revel in the thought of bringing a child happiness—it might also be a good idea to leave a note on the toy that lets people know they can take it. For example: "Take me home—I'm yours!"

May 25:
Be a Compassionate Clipper

Leave extra coupons on the shelf next to the item they are for. Easy peasy!

May 26:
Yes, You Can

Remove the word *can't* from your vocabulary and think about what is actually holding you back—fear, reluctance, pride? Once you stop talking yourself out of taking a risk or making a difficult decision, life will open up for you and so will your mind.

Do something nice and helpful without being asked. Take out the trash, clean the house, and visit a relative. Once you make a habit of these tasks, you won't need reminding since you will want to do them as you go about your usual day.

May 27:
Start a Changepot

This is exactly as it sounds: a pot for change. If you don't mind stopping in the middle of a sidewalk or side of the road, pick up loose change that has fallen to the ground. Add your findings to the same pot and after a few months, see how much you have collected. If you're strapped for cash, spend your findings on a nice meal for your family. If you are fairly stable financially, donate the money (anonymously) to a good cause.

May 28:
Wish Upon a Hero

Grant someone a wish through Wish Upon a Hero, a network dedicated to people helping people. Anyone can be a hero by sending a donation or offering a service. Explore heronetwork.com to browse through wishes and see if you can help with any. It is a really good reminder of what others are going through and that you are needed in this world.

May 29:
Click to Give

There are many websites that are click-to-give. Just by clicking, you can help send food or money to countries and causes that need them. One of them is greatergood. com. It just takes a few keystrokes to make someone's life better.

May 30:
Have a Good Neighbor Policy

. . . .

If you live next to an elderly couple or someone who is disabled, volunteer to help them around their yard by raking their leaves or mowing their lawn. Consider it good exercise and a good deed.

May 31:
World No-Tobacco Day

. . . .

Smoking is a drag, literally. It is bad for your health and the environment. If you need a little push to help you quit or to encourage a loved one to stop smoking, the American Lung Association website at lung.org is replete with helpful information. They report that smoking-related diseases in the United States claim an estimated 443,000 lives each year. In addition, cigarette smoke contains over 4,800 chemicals, 69 of which are known to cause cancer. Leave this old habit behind and we'll all breathe easier!

chapter six

June

Everything Under the Sun

All the flowers of all the tomorrows are in the seeds of today.

—INDIAN PROVERB

June 1:
Live Aloha

In the beautiful paradise known as the Hawaiian Islands, there is a tradition of "Living Aloha." In Hawaiian culture, *aloha* includes the concepts *akahai, lokahi, olu`olu, ha`aha`a,* and *ahonui*—in English, these words translate to kindness, bringing unity, politeness, humility, and enduring. If you live your life with simple acts of goodness every day and follow the tradition of native Hawaiian islanders, you will surely become a good in the world.

June 2:
A Bagel and a Hug

It's easy to feel overwhelmed from everything that life throws your way. If you notice a friend or coworker struggling, be there for them. Bring them a bagel or coffee, or something simple to show them that you care. Take their mind off of their challenges, if only for a moment.

June 3:
Friends Let Friends Forage

Plant a fruit tree. We know trees clean air by absorbing odors and pollutants while also providing oxygen and shade. And if you want to be generous, go ahead and plant a fruit tree near the fence or street. Put up a little sign that says "Help yourself!"

June 4:
Agree to Disagree

Respect the choices of others. We may not always agree with our loved ones, but increase peace by respecting their decisions and being there for them regardless. If everyone thought alike, think how boring it would be. Our differences enrich our lives, and all the more so when handled respectfully.

June 5:
It's the Thought that Counts

Leave something useful in an area where it will most be needed: an umbrella next to a public doorway or a spare bag at the grocery store for those who forgot theirs. Practice tiny acts of kindness!

June 6:
Catch People Doing Something Right
(and Make Sure They Know It)

During difficult transitions, our natural tendency is often to resist change and grow rigid. In this state, we seem to only be able to focus on the negatives. We think about the despair that follows the death of a loved one, but not the wonderful moments spent together. We think of the heartbreak of a relationship ending, but not of the exhilaration and freedom of being unattached. We might even scold our loved ones, or our friends, or coworkers for something minor when we ourselves wallow in similar negativity. But it is in these moments that gratitude can be used to alter this way of thinking.

Finding positives and accentuating them is the easiest way to turn those proverbial frowns upside down and gray skies back to blue. Try catching someone doing something right for a change, not something wrong. Giving praise for a job well done will lift all parties involved.

June 7:
Be Kind to Yourself, Too

Make a commitment to refrain from negative self-talk. Be kind to yourself and focus on the traits you like, rather than the ones you don't. The extremely wise Dawna Markova, the author of a favorite book, *I Will Not Die an Unlived Life*, says "Your soul remembers when you put yourself down; it imprints upon you. Never do this. Self-compassion is key to a life well-lived."

June 8:
Birthday Girl

Give your mom a present on your birthday. She gave you the gift of life, and this is a sweet acknowledgment of her labor.

June 9:
Honor Abused Women and Children's Awareness Day

Collect coupons for life's little essentials, buy the merchandise, and then donate them to a homeless shelter or a home for abused women and children. I donate magazines and books to my shelter of choice, the fantastic Delancey Street (delanceystreetfoundation.org). They have been making a difference in people's lives for decades and turned thousands of lives around.

June 10:
Give Your Old Clothes a Promotion

Donate your unworn, professional clothing to dressforsuccess.org. This organization promotes economic independence for disadvantaged women by providing them with clothing they can wear to work, thereby advancing their career and confidence.

June 11:
Save Somebody's Life in Just One Second

If you have a driver's license, choose "yes" when you're asked to become an organ donor.

June 12:
The Good Neighbor Policy

Bring your neighbor's newspaper to their front door and leave a plate of homemade muffins next to it.

June 13:
Phoning It in for a Good Cause

Donate your old cell phone to the National Coalition Against Domestic Violence (ncadv.org). They will donate the proceeds to programs that protect families who have suffered abuse.

June 14:
The Good Old Days and the Good New Days

Share happy memories. Keep in touch with a friend by sending an old photo to them via snail mail and write a short note about the day it was taken on the back of the photo.

June 15:
Dad's Big Day

On July 19, 1910, the governor of the state of Washington proclaimed the nation's first Father's Day. However, it was not until 1972, 58 years after President Woodrow Wilson made Mother's Day official, that the day became a nationwide holiday in the United States. Celebrate your father today by making him feel special and loved with a homemade gift or meal. For your friends who may have lost their father, check in with them as this day may be difficult. Perhaps you can connect them with the many "rad dads" at senior centers who are elders with wonderful stories and few family members.

June 16:
Rewire Your Brain to Be More Positive

Neuropsychiatrist David Amen, MD, posits that thoughts carry physical properties and that the properties of negative thoughts can be detrimental to leading a healthy, happy life. To overturn these negative effects, he prescribes thinking more positively so you can change the way your brain works and in turn change your life for the better.

June 17:
Love the Ones You're With

I have seen this excellent exercise put into practice at work, family reunions, and dinner parties. It never fails to bring a group of people closer, and it brings out the best in anyone. Call everyone to attention and say you want to acknowledge your appreciation for the group. Time your moment well—whenever there is a lull in conversation would be best and never at the beginning of a get-together.

Here are some examples:

> *"What I appreciate about Julian is his humility; he is brilliant but never showy."*

> *"What I appreciate about Leslie is her kindness and generosity. She helped me out when I was in a bad way. I will always be grateful to her for that."*

Offer a positive appreciation for each person and encourage others to do the same. Talk about a turnaround! This can turn stormy skies blue in five minutes flat.

June 18:
Mindful Memo
. . . .

Write a note of gratitude to the people in your everyday life who make a difference—the mailman, a grocery clerk, or the greeter at the mall. Tell your friends about their great service so their businesses can grow. Just by paying attention to those who can so easily go unnoticed (especially if your smartphone is glued to your hand), you can enrich each other's lives a little each day.

June 19:
Teach Your Children Well
. . . .

Sit down with your child and ask them to start a discussion about thankfulness. Provide a simple starting point: "Thank you for..." Then ask your child to draw a picture to go with the concept and get started writing the first of *many* thank-you notes for years to come!

June 20:
Pay It Forward

Stop for a moment and think of someone who needs a gesture of kindness. Perhaps it is something kind that someone once said to you. With gratitude for what was given, reach out and give back. It can be a simple gesture, like sending a card, or calling someone who is sick and saying you care. You may well recall the movie or book, but if you want ideas and to connect to other kindly folks, go to payitforwardfoundation.org. *Pay It Forward* is about all people, from all walks of life, giving to others and making a positive difference. At last count there were more than 500,000 people in 60 countries around the world participating.

June 21:
Be More Thoughtful

You know your coworker works really hard and can come in a bit bedraggled at the end of an arduous week. Why not walk up to her, say, "Good Morning!," and hand her a vitamin-rich protein smoothie or fresh hand-pressed juice?

June 22:
Be That Helping Hand

Every Sunday night, when you go to take out your own garbage and recycling, knock on your neighbor's door and offer to take hers out, too. You might even be invited in for tea and cookies, as I was!

June 23:
Talk Less, Listen More

Listening is one of the greatest gifts you can give anyone. As humans we all want to be heard, so start by listening a little more each day. Listen to your children, your spouse, your friends, even the Chatty Cathy in the office. You, in turn, will be repaid by being listened to with far more attention and care.

June 24:
Simple Acts of Goodness

Get acquainted with the power of simple human kindness and easy acts of goodness every day. When at the grocery store, return the cart or help the elderly man struggling with his bags. Open doors for people. Say "Hello" with a smile. Every day and in every way choose to take the high road in your travels. The view is much more beautiful from up top!

June 25:
Be the Light in Dark Days

Sometimes we all feel deflated or overwhelmed, someone hurts us or disappoints us, or we hear bad news about a loved one's medical condition. On those days, when you feel your light has gone out, remember there is always a glimmer of hope and something to be thankful for. Albert Schweitzer said it well: "Sometimes our light goes out, but is blown again into instant flame by an encounter with another human being. Each of us owes the deepest thanks to those who have rekindled this inner light."

June 26:
Don't Just Go Through It, *Grow* Through It

· · · · · · · · · · · · ·

An attitude of gratitude can make a profound difference in our day-to-day lives. Yet, as we all come to know, not every day is filled with good things. We each endure difficult passages: illnesses, money trouble, work woes, relationship issues, the loss of a loved one, and countless others. These are the vicissitudes of life. However, it is the attitude you bring to each situation that makes all the difference. Share what you learned from others during these life lessons and offer help to a fellow traveler who is walking a hard path.

June 27:
Service

"To Be of Use," Marge Piercy's marvelous poem, suggests something of the human condition—that we all long to be useful, to help, to work together toward a common goal. This is surely the best part of the human spirit. Meditate upon this:

What is my true purpose? What am I here to do in this life?

I recommend that you contemplate this question deeply and for a very long time—days, weeks, months, and years even. Let the answer speak through your service to others.

June 28:
Get Out of Your Head and Back Into Your Heart
. . . .

Because the world we exist in today is very much about staying in your head, many of us have to make a concentrated effort to become grounded and in touch with our bodies and the natural world around us. Grounding is a technique for centering yourself within your being. Grounding is the way we can reconnect and balance ourselves though the power of the element of earth. When you see someone driving past talking on their cell phone, you know that they are not grounded. For deep grounding, we recommend a creative visualization or, better yet, a group guided meditation.

This is the simplest of rituals, one you can do every day of your life. As you walk, take the time to look and really see what is in your path. For example, my friend Eileen takes a bag with her and picks up every piece of garbage in her path. She does this as an act of love for the Earth. During the ten years she has practiced this ritual, she has probably turned a mountain of garbage into recycled glass, paper, and plastic. Eileen is *very* grounded. She is also a happy person who shares joy with all in her path.

June 29:
Your Goals Will Grow You
. . . .

Make a list of short-term goals you would like to achieve by the end of the year, month, or even week. As you accomplish your goals, give gratitude for the effort, inspiration, people, and other factors that helped you along the way. My goal is to see how I can give more to those around me, near and far. I would love to hear your aspirations!

June 30:
A Litter of Love
. . . .

June is the ASPCA's Adopt-A-Shelter-Cat month. Millions of cats roam our streets. Some are looking for a kind person to take them in and give them a new home. This population swells at this time of year since shelters are overflowing with all the kittens born during the springtime. Shelter cats make excellent companions. However, just as cats give people love and companionship, humans need to care for their cat and provide her with an appropriate loving home. Careful research and planning is the key to adopting the right cat for your family, since adopting one should never be an impulse decision and indoor felines can live up to 20 years.

chapter seven

July

The Beauty and Bounty of Summer

Kind acts come from a place within that we all have inside us. Sometimes we just need a reminder of the unlimited power of the human heart.

—WILL GLENNON

July 1:
Trees Are the Lungs of Our Planet

Have you heard about the amazingly ambitious goal of the Nature Conservancy to plant a *billion* trees and restore the forests of the world? From the rainforests in South America to China and even in the Arctic Circle, this hardy group of tree huggers is doing their darndest to recreate the woodlands and rainforests everywhere they can. I urge you to look at the map to see how far they are getting. It is impressive and gives me so much hope about our future.

July 2:
I Think I Shall Never See Anything as Beautiful as a Tree

I grew up in a deeply forested state, West Virginia, and was taught from childhood to know and love trees. The last time I visited, as I drove all around to see relatives in far-flung counties, I noticed huge swaths of brown amongst the green. I asked what the heck was going on that seemed to be killing trees. That is how I learned about acid rain, an unfortunate by-product of coal mining, logging, and too many chemical plants. On our 300-

acre farm, no trees are cut, only planted, so we are doing our part.

In the settled part of the great prairies and western states, trees were felled to clear the land. That is, in part, being rectified by a special effort to protect trees in the last frontier. Check out americanforests.org to see how you can help. Oh, and start in your own yard. Got room for a couple of trees? Start digging and planting and know you will enjoy years of beauty and leave behind a legacy for generations to come from your own efforts.

July 3:
Shed and Help Others Get Ahead

I bet you have too many shoes. I do, and I really only like a few pairs that are comfy and look good, too. Donate your unused, new and gently used footwear to soles4souls.org and you will help somebody who needs them more than you do. Many of these go to folks looking to rejoin the workforce who need nice interview shoes and on-the-job kicks, too.

July 4:
Do You Know How Great You Are?

Compliment someone today, and mean it. A genuine compliment can boost someone's confidence and that is a great feeling. If you like your coworker's blouse or new haircut (or both!), tell her. Open and honest communication works wonders for developing relationships and makes everybody's day a little bit nicer.

July 5:
Glad Days

Let someone know that you appreciate having him or her in your life. Sometimes we forget how good it feels to be appreciated; yet we know how lousy it feels to be unappreciated. Go ahead and tell someone how thankful you are for his or her presence; it will only make you closer.

July 6:
Tell the Truth

Be truthful, even when it is hard. If someone asks for your opinion, give it honestly. Otherwise, you can't be confident in your own answer. My friend Nancy Fish lives by this and one other ideal (more about that later!).

July 7:
Acknowledge Excellence

Did you have a helpful or enthusiastic waiter at the last restaurant you went to? Call and tell the manager about the great experience you had. Do you still think about a college professor that impacted you? Write them a letter to thank them. Many jobs are thankless jobs, so remember how good it feels to be thought of and appreciated, even years later. Also, telling your friends and family about your good experiences with these people can help their business flourish.

July 8:
Treats for the Sweet

Treat someone to a meal—this is especially effective when people least expect it! Whether you are out with a friend or see a person in need on the street, take the opportunity to buy their meal without offering. Just do it.

July 9:
Book 'Em

Give a book to someone out of the blue. Consider their interests and buy them a book. Recently, one of my friends said she wanted to cook more at home instead of eating out most nights. I got her two cookbooks on one-pot meals and slow cooker recipes. Much to my surprise and delight, she's been sharing some delicious soups and stews she discovered in her reading, and sharing these makes for truly high-quality time together.

July 10:
Show Someone You Care

Collect or buy some items to make a care package for someone, such as a soldier serving overseas or a child in need you have found through an agency. I have two shelves in my closet where I stash stuff I know will make a difference in someone's day. I picked up this wonderful habit from my mom and the ladies at her church. They have the knack of knowing just what people want.

July 11:
Green Day

If you are able to, walk or ride your bike to school, work, or wherever you need to go. By not using a car, you are helping to reduce greenhouse gases while burning some calories at the same time! You can also use public transit or carpool with a friend—this also gives you the golden opportunity to bond with your coworkers or get to know more about your friend.

July 12:
Tend Your Garden

Grow your own garden, even it is just on a stoop, window-sill, or fire escape. Fruits, vegetables, and herbs, oh my! Think of the recipe possibilities if your ingredients were right in your own backyard. Growing your own produce can save you money and time spent picking through the bruised and aged produce some grocery stores offer. This is also a great way to go organic!

July 13:
Gaggles for Good

Plan an outing with a group of friends that will positively impact society. Instead of just going to the movies again, gang up for the good of all. Together, plant a community garden, help clean up a schoolyard, or volunteer for a nonprofit organization. In the San Francisco Bay Area, there are regular beach clean-up efforts and it is enormously rewarding to see the unmarred beauty beneath the trash. Find your local chapter of "Heal The Bay," and get a little sun, sand, and healing for you, your friends, and your closest coast.

July 14:
Learn the Art of Letting Go

After all, we are all human and we have a little baggage (or a lot)! Sometimes I hold in my feelings until they are like a dam about to overflow. Luckily for me, I have had the opportunity to learn from great authors like Sue Patton Thoele, Melody Beattie, and Mark Nepo that we just have to move on toward the positive. Release any repressed anger and pain that you have been keeping inside. Allow yourself to let go of the past so that you can proceed to live in the present without worry, fear, or resentment. Remember that this isn't a one-time event, but a process. Letting go is an act of kindness for yourself. Once you can accept that life isn't always something you can predict or control, yours will eventually become more positive and joyous.

"I've learned that no matter what happens, or how bad it seems today, life does go on, and it will be better tomorrow."

—MAYA ANGELOU

July 15:
Add a Half Hour to Your Day

One of the most brilliantly simple pieces of advice I ever heard was from Peter Shankman at a publishing conference. He said it had transformed his life and it is simply this: get up a half hour earlier and use that to reach out to people. He said it can be as easy as wishing a happy birthday to your Facebook contacts, one meaningful phone call first thing in the morning, or writing a personal note to someone you have been meaning to be in contact with. I remember listening to him and thinking I really didn't want to get up any earlier. My days were long enough (see July 14 on letting go—clearly I needed to do some right then!) and that did not sound appealing. But his sincerity and enthusiasm somehow broke through my "baditude" and I pondered the idea as I walked back to my car and drove across the Bay Bridge back to my office. I decided to try it and I can tell you, he is *right*.

The extra half hour of every morning has been one of the best investments I ever made, and so much so that I added an hour. It completely changed my life for the better. Try it!

July 16:
Show a Little Tenderness

Let public workers know that they're doing a good job. (See July 15, and try using a few minutes of your extra half hour to write thank-you notes to your local police station. I imagine it happens *very rarely*.) When you see a fire truck, ambulance, school bus, or police car, go ahead and thank the workers inside for their hard work. Whether internally thought or externally voiced, this appreciation goes a long way.

July 17:
Think "Best Case Scenario" All the Time

Many people overanalyze situations, psych themselves out, and only consider the worst-case scenarios. I, for one, am guilty as charged. Let's start each day on a positive foot and make a list of your "best-case scenarios." What are the best things that could possibly happen to you? To your family? To the world? Have fun with this and think big!

July 18:
Each One, Teach One

Spread around a love of literature, books, and writing! Many children and some adults struggle when it comes to reading. Look into volunteering for adult literacy classes or reading to the elderly at a retirement home at proliteracy.org, an organization with an amazing legacy: Laubach Literacy International's history began in 1930, when Dr. Frank C. Laubach was a missionary among the Maranao people of the Philippines. His concern about their poor living conditions led him to conclude that the ability to read and write was essential for them to begin to solve their problems. As the Maranaos learned to read, they would, in turn, teach other adults on a one-to-one basis that became known as "Each One, Teach One." From 1935 to 1967, Dr. Laubach visited 105 countries, answering calls for literacy help and creating reading lessons in 315 languages.

July 19:
Stop Interrupting Others When They Are Speaking

We have become a nation of interrupters, as though what we have to say is more important than anyone else's opinion or thoughts. Think before you speak. If a friend is confiding in you, consider if your words can truly help them. Many people interrupt or relate the problem back to themselves instead of thoughtfully responding to the person who is confiding in them. Reflect on what you have heard and then reply. This is not only basic manners but also means a lot to the person to whom you are listening. I guarantee you will start to notice when you are interrupted once you have stopped. Listening is an act of love.

July 20:
Dryers Are Energy Vampires—
Clotheslines Are Better

Hang dry your wet laundry. By doing so, you're saving energy and preserving the fit and color of your clothes!

July 21:
Your Conscience Will Be Cleaner!

Save water by taking shorter showers.

July 22:
Spend Your Money in Your Own Neighborhood

Support local agriculture and business by purchasing produce or baked goods from farmer's markets. By doing so, you ensure that your fresh food is organically grown and isn't imported from another state or country—the cost of shipping is a contribution to greenhouse gas and pollution. Every dollar you spend locally will go a long way toward supporting your local economy *and* your next-door neighbors.

July 23:
Save Rare Earth

Cell phones and batteries are some of the largest contributors of toxic substances to our landfills. More than 13 million cell phones become obsolete in California every year, and historically only seven percent have been recycled. Over 80% of reusable batteries are composed of the hazardous heavy metals nickel and cadmium. Mobile phones contain hazardous levels of lead, nickel-cadmium, and other toxic materials. While these and other rechargeable batteries have been banned from disposal in California for several years, recycling opportunities have lagged. According to Californians Against Waste, for every million cell phones we recycle, 35,000 pounds of copper, 772 pounds of silver, 75 pounds of gold, and 33 pounds of palladium can be recovered. Go to epa.gov for more information on how to recycle your cell phone.

July 24:
Step Up

Challenge yourself. Life is a process and throughout your years on this planet, get to know yourself better at every stage. Surprise yourself. If you go through life without trying something new, you are not doing yourself justice. Discover your true potential and maybe more than just your life will improve.

July 25:
Kicks for Kids

Next time you are in the mall or wandering the web doing some retail therapy, buy a gift card from Nordstrom's in support of the Shoes That Fit program. For as little as ten bucks, you can donate a pair of brand new tennies that fit perfectly for a young person who needs a leg up. Check out shoesthatfit.org. The right shoes can be the first step in the right direction.

July 26:
Night Time Is the Right Time

If you think back to your childhood, I bet a favorite plush toy or a "blankie" is involved. The safety and comfort you and I might have enjoyed are not guaranteed for all, so let's blanket children with love. A donation of $25 to Project Night Night (projectnightnight.org) funds a nice tote bag with a blankie and a book by a top children's author for a homeless child.

July 27:
Good Night, Moon. Good Morning, Sunshine!

I have to agree with the lovely people of the Pajama Program (pajamaprogam.org) that the sweeter side of life comes from warm, snuggly PJs so I love their mission—to provide pajamas and a book of bedtime stories to children who need them. Need I say more?

July 28:
Blanket the World With Love

Do you remember Linus of the venerated *Peanuts* cartoon? His love for his blanket shows how universal that love for just the right soft cloth can be. My mom and aunts are amazing quilters. They can seemingly take anything and make a gorgeous, collectible quilt from it. Even if you, like me, lack that "quilting gene," you can blanket the world with your love and good intentions by collecting them for donation. I put out a call and got a ton of nice comforters to donate to Project Linus, at projectlinus.org. This nurturing organization sends cozy quilts and oh-so-warm blankets to kids in shelters, hospices, hospitals, and wherever the cloaking comfort of love might be needed. My mom recently made a quilt of some of my crazy outfits from the eighties, so I can only hope that the beneficiaries of Project Linus have a good sense of humor and a love of neon colors!

July 29:
Teach What You Know
· · · · · · · · · · · · ·

My family frequently wondered what I would ever do with an English degree. One of many things I've done is mentor a student in grammar and hopefully foster a love of reading, the benefits of which will last a lifetime. Check out the vast array of opportunities to teach and to learn at teachforamerica.org.

July 30:
Cartloads of Kindness
· · · · · · · · · · · · ·

This one is so simple that I really shouldn't have to write it here, but you'd be surprised how many people don't put their shopping carts away once they are done unloading their groceries! Walk the extra ten feet to the nearest shopping corral and roll that cart on in. Done! In addition, if you notice someone about to put their cart away and you need one, offer to take their shopping cart. These momentary connections that can happen in the frozen food aisle or parking lot are good for us. Keeps us human. Keeps us together.

July 31:
Get. Very. Simple.

. . . .

I once had the pleasure of attending a lecture by Huston Smith, the preeminent scholar of the world's religions. (He first came to global attention when he brought a young Tibetan Buddhist Monk—His Holiness, the Dalai Lama—to America for the first time.) Smith spoke about the continuing impact of religion on our world, most notably the strife all around the word over religious differences. He was at his most joyous when he spoke about his own spiritual practices, which he described to us. Smith said, upon rising each day, he did Hatha yoga, followed by reading a few pages of a sacred text, after which he meditated or prayed for at least five minutes. He would finish his morning ritual by doing a bit of yard work and some composting, which results in rich, dark soil, and a beautiful garden he greatly enjoys.

The entire audience smiled as they listened to this great and humble man describe the simple spiritual practices that began each of his days. These were Huston Smith's personal morning rituals. I loved the irony that this premier academic, who has such a deep understanding of religious rituals throughout history, had created such an uncomplicated practice for himself. I left the talk inspired to worry less and enjoy more. I saw the deep wisdom of simplicity.

I recently saw him again at San Francisco's esteemed California Institute of Integral Studies and heard the one detail he had left out of the previous discussion of morning practices. That night, Huston introduced a dear old friend, who added this delightful detail he knew from their time as college roommates: upon waking, Huston sits up ramrod straight in his bed, claps his hands together, and says very loudly, "It's going to be a GREAT DAY!"

chapter eight

August

Book Your (Volunteer) Vacation

Live with intention. Continue to learn. Do what you love. Live as if this is all there is.

—MARY ANNE RADMACHER

August 1:
Slow Down

. . . .

Take it easier. There is a lot of hustle and bustle in this world, and it's easy to miss the simple joys of life if you are always in a hurry. Alter your perspective a bit and take your time. When grocery shopping, instead of rushing through your list, walk down every aisle, notice all the colorful fruits and vegetables, enjoy this errand, and be grateful that you can afford to buy groceries.

Here is when you know you are going too fast: when you forget to be nice. When that happened to me, I took stock and realized I was heading in the wrong direction. Now I am doing my best to not do the crazy busy thing. It doesn't do any of us any good. Least of all me. Least of all you.

August 2:
Popcorn and a Movie

. . . .

Donate movies and toys to the children's ward at your local hospital. Even better, stay and watch a movie in the social room and bring doctor-approved treats!

August 3:
One Man's Scrap Is Another Man's Treasure

Redistributing surplus has been the driving force behind many nonprofit organizations serving local communities. One of my favorite initiatives is the Scroungers' Center for Reusable Art Parts, otherwise known as SCRAP. SCRAP has been operating in an industrial district in San Francisco since 1976. Donations of paper, paint, and all kinds of arty bits and pieces are the mainstay of SCRAP's inventory. I've seen reams of embossed ribbon, plaster casts, tubes of glitter, and circuit boards. They offer art supplies at very low cost and provide free materials for art projects. Go over there and get inspired to create! Learn more information about SCRAP, a source for the resourceful, at scrap-sf.org.

August 4:
Open Your Home

The gift economy is a really helpful concept for the budget-conscious, and it can help you, too. It may be time to reexamine everything you thought you couldn't do and see if there is another way. Vacationing is a good example—you can trade homes and explore what you could not afford before, while offering the same in return. This free accommodation exchange will give you a really unique and much more personal view of a new place as well as a way to connect with people who live there. The idea is not new; Servas International (servas.org) was founded in 1949 and is recognized by the United Nations as a hospitality network. Check out the wildly successful and well organized CouchSurfing (couchsurfing.org) and Hospitality Club (hospitalityclub. org). And take time to look around the web; there are many similar, smaller initiatives online catering to the budget traveler or people wanting to take a volunteer vacation in another hemisphere.

August 5:
Be an Anonymous Gifter

Have you heard about the Bolinas Free Box? This institution began 30 years ago by accident. As the story goes, a young couple was departing the shores of Bolinas, California, and dumped some boxes of extra belongings behind the community center as they left. The rather nice assortment of clothes, books, and household utensils drew some interested residents to have a look. By the end of the day, several other people had brought free stuff down to share. The Free Box took up residence in a shed between the health food store and the community center and has been providing all comers with all kinds of free fare ever since. The era of the free box was born.

August 6:
The Art of the Free

The free box is a very workable concept, as the longevity of the Bolinas Free Box attests, but there are problems to be avoided. Dropping off damaged, soiled, or unusable items is inappropriate. Also, tidiness must be taken into consideration. The best-case scenario is an organized walk-in so that people can see what freebies are available. A free box initiative really needs a shed or other weather-proof shelter that people can easily access, and committed volunteers are essential to keep the stock in reasonable order. It works the other way around, too, thanks to places like DonationTown.org, who will come and pick up stuff you are ready to "free up" into the world. After all, donating household items gives a second life to the things you no longer need.

August 7:
Become a Modern Digger

There is plenty of free stuff to be found in every community. Urban foraging, or dumpster diving, has become very popular in the last few decades. Well-known proponents of the movement include Food Not Bombs, which began feeding the hungry with salvaged food 30 years ago; and I first learned about The Diggers when I was interviewing the great poets Diane di Prima and Janine Pommy Vega for *Women of the Beat Generation*.

The Diggers, who came together in the sixties in San Francisco, regularly fed around 200 people a day on donated and foraged food. They also ran free shops, threw free parties, and started a free medical clinic.

Some contemporary urban foragers call themselves Freegans (a composite of *free* and *vegan*) and pride themselves on their recycling prowess. The Freegan mission is to live with minimal consumption of resources and limited involvement in the mechanisms of the conventional economy. If you fancy learning the skills necessary for successful dumpster diving, Freegans (freegan.info) are the people to contact. Active groups are listed, and some organize trash tours where they instruct newcomers on how to scavenge safely. The basic rules are commonsense: forage with at least one other person, always thoroughly check food when you get home and wash as needed before eating anything, and don't leave a big mess at the scene—the rodents will love you, but store owners won't!

August 8:
Make Sure Our Elders Are Well Fed

One in six Americans over age 60 faces the threat of hunger, and Meals on Wheels is there to help. A total of 2.5 million seniors in all 50 states, many of whom have chronic health conditions, rely on the service. Go to mowaa.org to make a one-time donation ($35 provides five meals), or join the Next Meal Club to donate monthly.

August 9:
Make Furry Friends

Studies show pets provide both a psychological and physical boost to their owners—so donate to petsfortheelderly. org to help a senior get a dog or a cat. The unconditional love of a pet can make a life that much sweeter.

August 10:
Help from Behind the Wheel
. . . .

Be a volunteer instructor in AARP's Smart Driver course (aarp.org/drive), which allows older drivers to brush up on their behind-the-wheel skills. Next time you want to give back, just put it in drive.

August 11:
#Helpful
. . . .

Are you software-savvy? Sign up to teach older adults computer and technology skills through SeniorNet (seniornet.org). Helping our elderly with tech skills is so rewarding. I have seen grandmothers go from never having emailed before to loving the world wide web and contributing their own wisdom, one tweet at a time.

August 12:
Letting Nothing Drop
. . . .

Sign up to volunteer with the anti-dropout program Communities in Schools (communitiesinschools.org), which helps vulnerable students in 26 states and the District of Columbia. Let's help get this to every state!

August 13:
Let Kids Be Kids

. . . .

Kids today play outside less than any previous generation. Promote play by donating to Ka-BOOM! (kaboom. org), a nonprofit that has built more than 2,300 playgrounds nationwide, to help make sure all children are within walking distance of a swing set.

August 14:
Go Back to School

. . . .

Give an elementary-school pupil who reads below grade level a leg up by tutoring them in biweekly 45-minute sessions through Reading Partners (readingpartners.org). Tutoring struggling readers is placing a bet on our future.

August 15:
Gifts that Give Back

. . . .

For every pair of thick and warm hand-knitted cable mittens purchased, CherryT Co. donates another pair to a child in need. Buying a pair at cherrytco.com is like sending out two big high-fives!

August 16:
Puppy Love

Show that *you* are well trained and buy a Kona Benellie blanket for your pup at konabenellie.com, and you'll also keep shelter dogs warm and cozy. Dog is your co-pilot, right?

August 17:
National Thrift Shop Day

Donate to and shop at thrift stores. You'll be recycling gently used items, supporting the local economy, and save money along the way. There are so many thrift stores working for charity but my favorite is this one in Denver that I discovered a couple of years while at a trade show: Denver-Cancer-Charity.org. What they are doing is *so* cool! The Cancer Cache Thrift & Gift Shoppe is operated as a not-for-profit charity that raises funds to provide free hats, wigs, scarves, and medical equipment to cancer patients. When I was undergoing treatment, I could never have afforded a wig or even a very nice hat, so these fabulous Rocky Mountaineers get my business every time.

August 18:
Life Is Too Short to Not Have Good Coffee

Get your next cup of joe and help orphans in Kamba, Kenya, with World Vision's 12-ounce whole bean coffee set, complete with a hand carved olive wood scoop. You can find it at worldvision.org.

August 19:
The Sweet Life

Show your support of childhood cancer patients and survivors with Lily's stevia-sweetened chocolate (lilyssweets.com). A portion of profits goes to nonprofits in Pennsylvania, California, and New York. Opening up a box of joy is good for us all!

August 20:
Guilt-Free Beauty

Be sure to buy beauty products that have not been tested on animals. Check with leapingbunny.org for a list of companies that do not test finished products, ingredients, or formulations on animals. You can also phone 1-888-546-CCIC (Coalition for Consumer Information on Cosmetics) and they'll be happy to send you a pocket-sized shopping guide of companies that manufacture with compassion. You can also look for the leaping bunny logo on cruelty-free products. Pretty on the outside and the inside!

August 21:
Compassionate Crafts

Some of my friends love to knit and crochet. Everyone I know has already had a colorful throw given to them, so what to do with the products of all that handwork? Look no further!

The Red Scarf Project (fc2success.org/how-you-can-help/red-scarf-project/) is looking for knitters to donate homemade red scarves for foster children in school. Whether you just learned to knit and purl or you are an expert, you can send encouragement and warmth to a foster student with a simple scarf.

Newborns in Need (newbornsinneed.org) would love clothing and bedding items for newborn, sick, needy, and premature babies. You can donate blankets, hats, booties, and afghans. All they ask is that you use the softest yarn possible.

Warming Families (warmingfamiles.webs.com) is a 100% volunteer-run project that delivers donated blankets and other warm items to the homeless and displaced. They supply to local shelters and nursing homes.

August 22:
Mindfulness at 55 MPH

Be a mindful driver, not a distracted danger to yourself and others. Driving, texting, and talking on the phone are very dangerous. Typing out a quick text may feel harmless, but texting requires visual, manual, and cognitive attention that you should be giving to the road. Think about—and educate yourself on—the dangers of distracted driving. Here are a few statistics provided by distraction.gov to get you started:

- An estimated 421,000 people were injured in motor vehicle crashes involving a distracted driver.
- 11% of all drivers under the age of 20 involved in fatal crashes were reported as distracted at the time of the crash.
- Sending or receiving a text takes a driver's eyes from the road for an average of 4.6 seconds, the

equivalent—at 55 mph—of driving the length of an entire football field, blind. Bottom line: don't do it!

August 23:
Be a Kid for a Day

Remember the good ol' days when you had more art projects than responsibilities? You can still embrace your inner child by spending the day with a young relative or your own child while playing games, making crafts, and encouraging creativity. You may reawaken talents and interests you had long since forgotten and introduce your child to new ones along the way. Paint a picture together, read storybooks aloud, play dress up and talk with them. This will create a strong bond between you two that will last a lifetime and make for great memories. Time is the most precious resource and spending it with a young person will have lasting, positive results on their life.

August 24:
Rice Is the Grain that Feeds the World

Rice is the grain that feeds more people in the world than any other, going back many thousands of years—to 6,000 BC in Northern Thailand, 5,000 BC in Northern India, and 10,000 BC in Kashmir. It is grown in paddy fields (water-filled beds) in countries all over the world—India, China, Indonesia, Thailand, Japan, the US, Greece, Turkey, and others.

There are so many wonderful ways to use rice that you could cook a new recipe per day for the rest of your life and not run out. Just be sure to use the correct rice type for the recipe or the dish will not be successful. For example, risottos need Arborio rice, a fat, starchy grain, which cooks to a soft, creamy texture yet retains a firm middle. Jasmine is aromatic rice and used in Thai cooking: it is a long grained yet sticky rice that remains moist and tender. Don't be afraid to make mistakes. Just learn how to cook each type, use a heavy pan, and don't overcook—or buy a rice cooker.

August 25:
Turn Off Your TV and Turn Your Brain Back On

Nowadays, children have computers and chat rooms, mobile phones, and a TV in their room with hundreds of channels in glorious color. Children can be techno-wizards—but TV is a time filler and time killer. It both encourages and normalizes violence, in both behavior and attitude. TV makes children lazy, and sluggish in thought and action.

If you feel your children are watching too much television and it's having a negative impact:

- Have all cable disconnected.
- Remove all TVs except one from the house.
- Limit TV viewing to set hours, such as only after homework is finished; and no TV during meals and no morning TV.
- Limit channels watched.
- Have family evenings that are fun. Encourage new hobbies.
- Don't rely on the TV for entertainment. Make your own. Talk to your family, and have them talk to you.

August 26:
Lighten the Load Laundry Has on Our Environment

Laundry can be a costly business, both financially and environmentally. Expensive conventional detergents and laundry aids are mostly derived from petroleum and often contain chemical fragrances and phosphates, which are known to deplete water of oxygen. This has devastating effects on fish—they basically starve and die. Eco-alternatives are much cheaper, just as effective, and so much better for our world.

At the store, look for phosphate-free, eco-friendly laundry detergent powder. The green brands use a soap base instead of petroleum, which works just as well without the deadly chemicals. You may even find that strange allergies and discomfort goes away as you eschew heavily chemical-laden soaps.

August 27:
Keep Your Garden Green

* Plant some bamboo. Bamboo contributes to the balancing of oxygen and carbon dioxide in the atmosphere.

- Don't use a leaf blower. The horrible noise is reason enough to avoid these machines. Compost instead, and never burn leaves!
- Plant a garden using xeriscaping—no water needed. Find out more at ecolife.com/garden/natural-lawn/xeriscaping.html.
- Capture rainwater for gardens.
- Fertilize with grass clippings.
- When watering your garden, turn on the water early in the morning to minimize evaporation.
- Try not to fertilize before a storm to avoid the fertilizer being washed away.

August 28: Be Generous

True generosity, with no strings attached, expecting nothing in return and without scorekeeping, is a direct expression of abundance. Be generous with your time and skills by volunteering for something you believe in; leave an extra tip for the wait staff; give away thank-you notes. Go through your closet and gather up things you don't wear and donate them to a homeless shelter or people in need.

August 29:
Serve the Public Servants

. . . .

Bake some goodies to take to your local police department, fire department, or teacher's lounge as a way of saying "Thanks!" They are your neighbors, too.

August 30:
Pass on the Pleasure of Reading

. . . .

Drop off your old magazines at a retirement home, hospice, or other place where the residents or patients may enjoy them. At my place of work, we get large-print copies of our books sent in multiples, so we keep one for our library, send one to the author, and share the others with our local retirement home. An elder Beat poet lives in the El Cerrito village for seniors, so I can drop off a collection of magazines and large-print books and then sit down for tea and a nice chat. I leave having received much more than I brought with me.

August 31:
Care Package

Instead of throwing old luggage away, donate your used suitcases and roller bags to foster homes. The children there often pack their clothes in garbage bags. Contact Family Services in your county to ask how to donate.

chapter nine

September

Study How You Can Help the World

I learned the most from the times of great difficulty in my life. These hard times were my teacher and from them I learned my most important lesson—give back.

—RICHARD J. CHIN

September 1:
Ready for Anything
. . . .

Take a CPR class. You never know when you might be in a position to put those life-saving skills into practice. Visit heart.org to find out where you can take a class. Being prepared to save a life is smart and a *big* good.

September 2:
Tithing
. . . .

I witnessed my mother tithe at church when I was a child and noted she did so with pride. I was also not unaware that she "did without" and forewent buying herself new purses or clothes. She was able to take care of my sisters and me while regularly giving her little bit of extra pocket money to the church. I learned about self-sacrifice and also about living from your values from her selfless actions.

Experiment with tithing. There is a universal law of tenfold return. This means that when you give freely, your return is tenfold. Particularly in terms of money, many of us think the law of attraction doesn't apply. It does. Money is simply energy, and when you allow the energy of abundance to flow through you, then money and other resources continue to flow to you. When you stop the flow of abundance out of fear, anxiety, and worry, the flow of money stops.

During the next six months, experiment. Whenever you get money, before you pay any bill, take ten percent and give it to something you believe in. What is most important is that you give with an open heart.

September 3:
Food and Shelter

Next time you do your grocery shopping, pick up a large bag of cat or dog food to donate to a local animal shelter. Your goodwill will be repaid to you with many loving licks.

September 4:
Go Ahead and Make Someone's Day

Some shops have punch cards that offer a free product after a certain amount of purchases. When you reach the limit before you get a free item, give the card to someone in line behind you and surprise them with a free coffee, frozen yogurt, or sandwich!

September 5:
Welcome Home, Baby (and Mom and Dad)

Make dinner for new parents the day they come home with their baby. Odds are they will be too busy and tired to cook dinner themselves. A healthy and delicious meal with plenty for leftovers can ease new parents back home and into their new routine.

September 6:
Don't Resent, Represent

Wash the dishes in your office kitchen. Your coworkers will notice that somebody did them and might return the favor of the anonymous example.

September 7:
Be Nice

Offer to help your roommate or spouse with one of their chores or do them entirely by yourself without anyone knowing. They will appreciate coming home to a vacuumed house or dinner already on the table. September is back-to-school and back-to-work time, and everyone is that much busier—so you should be that much nicer.

September 8:
Give 'Em Space

Leave the parking spot up front for someone else that might need to park closer than you do.

September 9:
A Quarter for Your Thoughts

If you see a car parked in a metered spot that is about to run out of time, slide in some loose change to help avoid a parking ticket. Sometimes the driver is just a few minutes late and a ticket is almost a 100% guarantee to spoil someone's good day.

September 10:
World Suicide Prevention Day

I think the tragic passing of transgender teenager Leelah Alcorn reminded us all about the need to be there for people, however we can. Volunteer for a crisis center or suicide hotline. So many people are in need of help, guidance, and support. Find a cause you are passionate about, or maybe even have a personal connection to, and spend some time actually helping with it. Volunteer Match (volunteermatch.org) takes your interests into consideration and matches you with a charity. We are all needed. Make it count.

September 11:
Pay Tribute

On September 11, 2001, America experienced a shocking and tragic loss that still reverberates. VOICES of September 11th provides information, support services, and annual events for 9/11 families, rescue workers, and survivors. Help commemorate this tragic day by helping organizations like VOICES to prevent acts of terrorism, improve responses to traumatic events, and promote resiliency to our nation. Visit voicesofseptember11.org for more information and learn how to become involved. We can learn from our history by honoring our past.

September 12:
Animals Have Rights, Too

Even with progressive legislation, our wildlife still faces a variety of threats. If it weren't for organizations like Defenders of Wildlife, I doubt almost any animals would be safe. Alaska's Arctic Refuge, the manatee, lynx, wolves, otters, and now the Endangered Species Act all are in harm's way.

On defenders.org, you can sign up for free wildlife updates, called Den Lines. Keep informed of any shenanigans going on and of how you can help, simply by using your mouse to make yourself heard. You can adopt an animal or two (adoption also makes a great gift!) or you can become a member and receive their excellent magazine. Defenders continue to need our support to carry on their fantastic work on our behalf...and on behalf of our wildlife and our wild places.

September 13:
Try Global Cooling, Instead

Scientists already know what is causing global warming and we are all contributing to it with our wasteful attitude and shortsightedness. We burn too much fossil fuel and massive deforestation of natural woodlands and forests continues unabated. Fossil fuels are pretty much pure carbon, laid down by the Earth over thousands and thousands of years. According to the folks at Environmental Defense, whenever you save energy—or use it more efficiently—you reduce the demand for gasoline, oil, coal, and natural gas. Less burning of these fossil fuels means lower emissions of carbon dioxide, the major contributor to global warming. Right now the US releases about 50,000 pounds of carbon dioxide per person each year. If we can reduce energy use enough to lower greenhouse gas emissions by about two percent a year, in ten years we will lose about 10,000 pounds of carbon dioxide emissions per person.

September 14:
Make a Social Call

Simply pick up the phone and call a good friend to talk about what is on your mind. Bare your soul; don't be afraid to ask for advice. Talk about what is going on in the world and what you can do about it. In this age of texting and Twitter, I have discovered the old-fashioned phone call is very welcome.

September 15:
How You Can Spare the Air

Here are some things that you can do starting today:

- Support our scientists by letting our elected officials know we need fossil fuel alternatives—wind power, solar power, and wave power.
- Choose more Earth-friendly transport, which also reduces smog-causing emissions.
- Recycle, conserve energy, and support the work of Environmental Defense and other environmental organizations.
- Go to environmentaldefense.org and get involved.

September 16:
Every Drop of Water Counts

We take water so for granted. We leave the faucet running when we brush our teeth, over-water our gardens, wash the car too often, take baths every evening rather than a quick shower, or don't mend that dripping tap. Become water-wise. At this writing, my landlord has not responded to my messages about the kitchen faucet dripping. So I have a bucket capturing it all in the sink and

I use that to water my backyard. I always have a bucket in the bathtub to capture shower water and haul it out to water my front and backyard. I used to get really strange looks from the neighbors but they are used to me now. A couple down the block started doing the same after we met at an afternoon block party!

September 17:
How to Be Water Wise

- One cup of water costs five times as much in a Nairobi slum as in an American city.
- Three gallons of water provide the daily drinking, washing, and cooking water of one person in the developing world...yet in the US, that flushes one toilet.
- Three gallons of water weigh 25 pounds. Women in Africa and Asia carry, on average, twice this amount of water over four miles...each and every day.
- 470 million people live in regions of severe water shortage. It's estimated, if nothing is done, that by the year 2025 this will increase six fold.
- Roughly one-sixth of our world's population does not have access to safe water.

❉ 2.5 billion people (roughly two-fifths of the world's population) do not have adequate sanitation according to the United Nations. 6,000 children each day die from unsafe water and sanitation: that is the equivalent of 20 jumbo jets filled with children crashing every day.

September 18:
Surf's Up

The Surfrider Foundation is an international nonprofit organization dedicated to the protection and enjoyment of the world's oceans and beaches through conservation, activism, research, and education.

Local chapters of this 19-year-old group work hard testing our oceans' water, cleaning beaches, campaigning, and visiting our schools for the benefit of all people, and hence marine life. The Surfrider Foundation distributes an excellent leaflet, "20 Ways to Cleaner Oceans and Beaches." Call 1(800) 743 SURF, or check surfrider.org for a copy.

September 19:
Think Good Thoughts

Each morning, I state the intention of my day by thinking about all the good things that are going to happen. I also think good thoughts for my friends and loved ones, especially those going through difficulty. It certainly doesn't cause any problems and I know it helps me, a lot.

September 20:
Power Your Life with the Positive

When life gets you down, remember to look on the bright side—and there is always a bright side. Be strong not just for yourself, but for those around you as well. Eleanor Roosevelt once said, "It is better to light a single candle than it is to curse the darkness." Look into the meaning of this quote: focus on the light in your life—and if there is none, try to be that light.

"Attitudes are contagious. Make yours worth catching."

—DAVID MEZZAPELLE

September 21:
Offer Unconditional Positive Regard

Be accepting. No matter a person's race, age, culture, or sexual orientation, accept everyone for who they are. Embrace the beauty of humanity and our myriad differences. By opening your eyes and mind to the possibility of love and friendship, new people will flow into your life and change your perspective in miraculous ways.

September 22:
National Car Free Day

Walk, bike, run, skip! Try not to drive as often. Put on your walking shoes and enjoy the area around you. Walk to the nearest convenience store if you need something or spontaneously visit a friend who lives close by. You may rediscover the beauty of your own neighborhood again in the process!

September 23:
Ain't No Mountain High Enough

Overcoming wilderness obstacles—rushing rivers, steep hills, avoiding wild animals—builds confidence and helps under-resourced kids better handle inner-city obstacles. All of this is why Big City Mountaineers pairs adults with disadvantaged youths on weeklong backpacking and canoeing trips. If you don't live in the regions where the organization primarily operates (Northwest, West and Midwest), check out Summit for Someone, a program that makes walk-a-thons look restful; participants fundraise for Big City Mountaineers by soliciting sponsorship for major climbing trips.

September 24:
Teach at Citizen School

Teach yoga, gardening, and more to middle schoolers. Reducing dropout rates by getting kids excited about learning is a major goal of Citizen Schools (citizenschools.org). Subjects covered in the 90-minute, 10-week after-school, volunteer-taught classes have included journalism, yoga, and architecture, with a focus on being "very interactive," says Stacey Gilbert, Director of Media Relations.

"Volunteers are encouraged to teach what they're passionate about."

September 25:
Give Someone's Grandfather or
Great Aunt What They Always Wanted

Grant a wish to a senior citizen. Volunteers for the Twilight Wish Foundation fulfill requests by donating items (like a home computer requested by a grandmother who wanted to email her grandkids) or by contributing their time. Learn all about it at twilightwish.org. Some wishes—like one from a retired postman who wanted to go over his old route one last time—require planning instead of money, and volunteers tend to choose items or actions that most speak to them.

September 26:
Friend a Family

Sponsor a low-income family via boxproject.org. The Box Project joins struggling families in depressed regions of rural America with individuals or groups who send about $50 worth of food, clothing, and medical supplies monthly. The idea is not just to provide financial support, but emotional support as well. Most participants develop long-term relationships over many years, cemented through letters. In addition, the organization encourages volunteers to learn about where the family they help lives, so they can impact public services and local policy. I know this is helping a lot of people in my home state of West Virginia where hard times remain.

September 27:
Take Care of the Planet

Each year, the National Environmental Education Foundation coordinates hundreds of events around the country on Public Lands Day. Volunteers are recruited to improve public parks and wildlife refuges by removing trash, planting trees, and doing other earth-friendly activities. Visit their website to find a service day near you: publiclandsday.org.

September 28:
Make Time for What Matters

Been meaning to spend more time with your family? Are you putting off errands? Is there not enough time to volunteer, go for a walk, or make dinner? Make time. Once you commit to something and begin to make a habit of it, you will be more likely to continue instead of saying, "I would like to, but I don't have enough time." You have the time; you just need to find it.

September 29:
Don't Be Idle

Turn off your car if you're going to be idle for more than 30 seconds (unless you are stuck at a red light). This will help save gas money, lessen air pollutants, and improve your car's fuel economy.

September 30:
By Your Hand

Use a dishwasher. This might surprise you, but washing dishes by hand uses six times as much water and twice the amount of energy as built-in dishwashers.

chapter ten

Share the Harvest

It is more blessed to give than to receive.

—ACTS 20:35

October 1:
Breast Cancer Awareness Month
. . . .

As we enter October, National Breast Cancer Awareness Month, be sure to schedule an appointment with your doctor to have an exam. Men need to remind their doctors, as well, as this is not just a women's issue. Remind your close friends to do the same and schedule appointments for the same time so you can go together and give moral support. It is important for us to be educated about all forms of cancer and to take the necessary steps to stay healthy. Visit breastcancer.org to answer any questions you may have.

I am a breast cancer survivor and deeply grateful. I remember getting the diagnosis and just going completely numb. I was like a zombie going through motions of my life, getting up and going to work, cooking dinner, trying to focus but all I could think was "I have cancer." My friends and family helped me through it all. I also had a genius doctor who got me and understood that it would be a physical, emotional, and spiritual journey. She was open to deep discussions about all that. I am lucky in so many ways, being free and clear for over a decade now. I bonded with my female physician, who asked me to stay

involved in her practice as a counselor for the newly diagnosed. I was honored. Each time I work with someone
who has just found out they have cancer, I offer my story
and all the success stories I have witnessed, while listening to their fears, dishing out lots of hugs, and helping
them in any way I can. This is one of the best things I do
with my life—using my wisdom to help another.

October 2:
Just Say Yes
. . . .

I (re)learned this truly vital lesson from *Imperfect Spirituality* author and blogger Polly Campbell: Once today, say "yes" to something unexpected that comes into your life.

Know that you are enough to handle whatever emerges from the yes. Know that you have the whole Universe supporting you. Believe that you will have a good time and learn something that you need to know. Exercise your faith by taking the Universe up on the good things that come your way and practice your optimism by believing that there is more to come. Just. Say. Yes. Then take two minutes to reflect and answer these questions for yourself:

- What did you say "yes" to today?
- Were you inclined to first say "no"? Why?
- How did you feel when you said "yes"?
- What did you learn about yourself by saying "yes" to this thing?
- What do you know now that you didn't know before you took the leap?

October 3:
World Smile Day!

Flash those pearly whites! Smile as you walk past someone. Maybe it's the barista handing you your much-needed double-shot latte in the morning, your neighbor planting flowers by their lawn as you go to check your mail, or a stranger walking their dog down the street. A simple, genuine smile can brighten someone's day as well as yours. It's really not that difficult to do. Remember that saying about it taking more muscles to frown than smile? Well, it's true!

October 4:
Do What You Say You're Gonna Do

Remember my friend Nancy Fish I mentioned a few pages back? This is the guiding principle of her life and it inspires me: *really commit*. Saying you'll do something and actually doing it are two very different things. Commit to something you've been meaning to do and take the first step today. If you don't, Nancy may track you down and hold you to it!

October 5:
Celebrate World Teacher's Day

Teaching others is hard work and can be a thankless job. Whether you are a student or have kids in school, approach a teacher and tell them what a great job they are doing. AdoptAClassroom.org goes to the head of the class in my book for the good work they do: it gives teachers a hand by providing needed classroom materials so that students can succeed.

It is estimated that more than 15 million children don't have the resources they need to do well in school. Teachers spend more than $1 billion a year stocking their own classrooms due to a lack of funding in schools. Supporting K–12th grade students in public, private, and charter schools, AdoptAClassroom.org makes it easy for donors to provide funding to classrooms throughout America. Teachers register their classrooms and needs online; donors discover classrooms through simple search tools, and make targeted contributions. Their goal is to connect donors with every classroom in the country. A-plus!

October 6:
Organize a Family Reunion
· · · · · · · · · · · ·

Get everyone together and spend the day at a park or one of your houses. Have a barbecue, play games, catch up on each other's lives. It's hard to stay in touch on a daily, weekly, or even monthly basis, so find a day where you can all reconnect. Set up a round-robin reunion so that everybody takes a turn and makes sure the closeness continues, year after year.

October 7:
Be a Tourist in Your Own Town
· · · · · · · · · · · ·

Go for a stroll around the city you live in. Pay attention to the little things you may have been missing, such as the architecture, the perfect picnic spot in a park, the greenery, and the people around you. Spend your money where your heart is, your own community.

October 8:
Giving Benefits the Giver, Too!

Find joy in giving. "Altruism boosts immune function, improves our moods, and is linked, not only to a higher quality of life, but a longer one," according to Stephen Post, at Stony Brook University. Those who help others also experience a "helper's high" when their bodies are flooded with feel good endorphins and other natural chemicals. It's pretty basic: when we do good, we feel good.

October 9:
Start Chatting It Up

My boyfriend has that magic ability to talk to anyone; 99% of the time, he makes a new friend, too. It is fun to watch him in action and he is definitely somebody you want to bring to parties and social occasions.

Be open to conversing with new people and becoming friendly with them. If you're at a bookstore and see someone holding a book you like, strike up a conversation and ask them about it. You may make a new acquaintance or find out that they're in the same business as you. You can network yourself, share ideas, and make connections at any time.

In line at the Pacific Café on Geary Street in San Francisco, we met a woman whose cousin from mainland China was being held in immigration detention for not having the proper paperwork. My boyfriend, who is fluent in Cantonese, was able to offer vital information to this family. You never know when *you* might need the help of a total stranger!

October 10:
Quit Feeling Sorry for Yourself

What follows is pretty much the best example of this I have ever heard (and deepest thanks to Polly Campbell for this astounding testament to the human spirit).

When Rhonda Sciortino was six months old, her mother left her at a neighbor's house and never returned. She was taken in by her grandfather, a mentally ill, depressed man who parented through abuse and neglect, and her grandmother, an alcoholic who ultimately drank herself to death. Life was filled with hunger, struggle, and pain. "I lived in a very dark place," Rhonda said. "Literally the house was dark, there were often no lights because the electric bill hadn't been paid. It was a filthy, oppressive place."

When she was about six years old, Rhonda was temporarily placed with a foster family who introduced her to the lighter side of life. "They lived in a clean house. There was plenty of food, they didn't fight with each other—I remember watching them interact with one another as though they really enjoyed being together," Rhonda, who is now 50, said. One day the man in the foster home encouraged her to search for the meaning in her own life. "Young lady," he said, "you better quit feeling sorry for yourself. You were put here for a reason, and you better be about finding out what it is." The family also took her to a Christian church, where Rhonda said, "meeting Jesus was a turning point."

Although she was ultimately placed back into the abusive home environment, Rhonda never forgot those people, their influence, or the role of Jesus Christ in her life. She believed that there was something more for her, something better. She discovered just what that was, when as an insurance professional, she received a thank-you note from the CEO of a children's home. She had helped the facility keep operating by saving it thousands of dollars in insurance premiums. For Rhonda, that thank-you note was infused with meaning. She quit her

job, and started her own insurance agency, founded sole-
ly to help the people and organizations that help children.
Today, she continues that work in her dream job as the
National Child Welfare Specialist for Markel Insurance
Company.

She lives with her husband of more than 20 years in
a light-filled home overlooking California's Pacific Coast
and she is a loving mother and grandmother.

Rhonda is no longer haunted by her darkness-filled
childhood, and no longer angry. "I've forgiven them for
the abuse and neglect," Rhonda said. "I value all my life
experiences, including the bad, because I gained an understanding and empathy that could not be acquired any
other way."

The resourcefulness, self-reliance, and persistence that
she developed to survive her childhood have also helped
her succeed in business and with her life's purpose.

October 11:
Pens Really Are More Powerful than Swords

Raise money for Pencils of Promise to help build a school in an impoverished country. For more information, visit their website: pencilsofpromise.org.

October 12:
A Friendly Eye

Offer to take care of a neighbor or friend's home, yard, or pets while they are away on vacation. They will be comfortable knowing their valuables are in good hands.

October 13:
Give Good Luck

If you see a penny on the ground, flip it to and make it face heads up. Some people find joy in picking up a lucky penny and you can help bring that joy to them.

October 14:
Develop More Patience

I love the old-fashioned ideas of virtues, such as kindness and generosity, *a lot*. I am determined to develop my patience muscle so it gets stronger all the time. Here is a big one for me: to learn to have patience with difficult people. (And realize I may be one myself and not know it!) This is not only a good deed for the person you are exhibiting patience towards, but it is also a good deed for yourself. Imagine that, a good deed for yourself!

For example, when someone pushes your buttons by doing something or saying something rude, you can choose to act with patience and understanding instead of anger. This will benefit you by keeping your blood pressure and stress levels low—which we know are two health issues that many people are suffering from today. My wise woman friend BJ Gallagher says, "Difficult people are the ones we learn the most from."

October 15:
DIY Optimism

Make a sign that reads, "Take what you need," with tear-off tabs on the bottom that say, "love," "courage," "optimism," and so on. Hang it up in places you regularly pass by. Keep refills at the ready!

October 16:
Feed a Family on World Food Day!

UNICEF works to give kids a healthy start and your contribution, large or small, can help someone on the other side of the globe. Go to UnicefUSA.org and explore all the options available to you.

Malnutrition is linked to nearly half of all childhood deaths. Children who are malnourished are smaller, more likely to get very sick from ordinary infections, and their brain development can suffer. By treating malnutrition in the first 1,000 days of a child's life, UNICEF has helped cut the number of children badly affected by over 100 million. Now that is making a difference on a global scale!

October 17:
Remember, It's Not All About You

Be punctual. Arrive on time to events. It's polite and professional, and you don't want to keep others waiting for you.

October 18:
No Gossip

Avoid listening to or spreading gossip. This is a really hard one in our tabloid society, but gossip is to be avoided. For one thing, it spreads negative energy all around. Say something nice instead. And mean it!

October 19:
Be Happy for Others (and Let Them Know It!)

When someone tells you their good news, be excited for them and show your enthusiasm. Sometimes we may envy the good things that happen to others. If you focus on how happy this person is, this will allow their joy to become yours as well.

October 20:
Turn Pain into Gold

. . . .

Everybody loves LL Cool J, but I love his wife, Simone I. Smith, even more. She is a cancer survivor who decided to give back in style: she teamed up with the American Cancer Society to introduce "A Sweet Touch of Hope," a lovely piece of jewelry which I proudly rock every day. Not only does it look really good, but this lovely lollipop charm helps raise funds and awareness to help save more lives from cancer, a disease that affects everyone in some way.

In 2004, Smith was diagnosed with Stage III chondrosarcoma—a very rare form of cancer. Her treatment required an invasive surgery that altered the appearance of a beloved lollipop tattoo. "It literally looks like someone took a bite out of it," she said. After her experience, Smith designed a lollipop line of jewelry that represents her journey to getting well and staying well. A portion of the proceeds goes to the Cancer Society, so Smith's inspired example can be an emblem of hope for every woman.

October 21:
Who Knew Compassion Could Be so Comfortable?

Buy a pair of Toms shoes. They are a one-for-one organization that donates a new pair of shoes to a child in need for every pair of Toms purchased. Visit toms.com to learn more about the cause and view the various styles. I like the shiny, glittery Toms!

October 22:
Go the Extra Mile

We have all needed help now and again, and maybe somebody spent time they didn't have in order to help us out. Return the favor and be that person who is prepared to walk an extra mile (maybe in Toms shoes!).

October 23:
More Beef=Fewer Trees

The next time you consider grabbing a burger at a fast-food place, remember this: over the past few decades, the rainforests have been disappearing to satisfy our hunger for cheap beef. Rainforests are home to over a thousand indigenous tribal groups, thousands of species of birds and butterflies and exotic animals—all of which are now endangered. Rainforests also affect rainfall and wind all around the world by absorbing solar energy for the circulation of our atmosphere. The trees provide buffers against wind damage and soil erosion, which then help prevent flooding along our coastlines. They are a precious part of our ecosystem. Let's all do something to protect them.

Over five million acres of South and Central American rainforests are cleared each year for cattle to graze on. The local people don't eat this much meat—it is exported to make the one dollar hamburger and a cheap barbeque meal.

October 24:
Recycling Saves the Rainforest

Here are some other things you can do to save the rainforest.

- Don't keep tropical birds or reptiles as pets. Let them live in nature.

- Buy items made from sustainable wood. Hardwood teak and rosewood encourage logging and deforestation.

- Recycle all your cans. Bauxite is mined from the ground in tropical countries and is the source for aluminum.

- Buy local, organic food whenever possible. Conventional agriculture is exhausting our forests' resources.

- Support any organization that is legitimately working to protect the environment in developing countries and in precious rainforests.

October 25:
National Forgiveness Day

If you have borne a grudge for someone, forgive them or let it go. You don't need that negative energy in your life. Remember that forgiveness is not absolution; what happened in the past still happened, but forgiveness can relieve yourself of the burden that has been weighing you down. Now you can heal. Our society is also in need of lessons in forgiveness and a dramatic reminder of this can be found in the film and foundation behind unlikelyfriendsforgive.com. They promote the real power of atonement and the art of forgiving, even after brutal acts of violence.

October 26:
Rescued Treasure

At the El Cerrito Recycling Center, they have a lively re-use center where you can donate things that are still viable to others. I have seen amazing donations like washers and dryers being hauled away by a family who could not have otherwise afforded a set. My favorite moment there was the time a donated sitar's new owner gave a free concert to all us recyclers.

October 27:
Walking Your Talk (I Am a Bag Lady)

● Keep a compact, reusable bag in your purse for those spur-of-the-moment purchases.

● Refuse a plastic bag for five items or less.

● Fit purchases from different stores into the same bag wherever possible. There's no reason to have eight shopping bags with only one item in each.

● Put your cloth bags back in your car as soon as you're done unloading groceries. There's less chance of forgetting them at home that way (and you'll be one step closer to using them!). Keep them on the front seat, rather than in the trunk. If you see them, you'll be far less likely to forget them.

October 28:
George Washington Liked Hemp,
So Why Shouldn't You?

Some eco-smart Canadians created a completely cool substitute for plastic wrap called Abeego. This hemp and cotton fabric is infused with a blend of beeswax, resin, and jojoba oil. It's flexible and able to stick to itself, and can seal bowls and wrap cheese, sandwiches, and snacks. It even looks good! Check it out for yourself at abeego.com.

October 29:
Saving the Planet One Paper Towel at a Time

Do you really need to use so many paper towels? One roll will last me at least a month at home. I have a whole shelf of well-used dish rags that started out their life as a nicely embroidered fabric and now are much more useful to me and the planet! Ditch the paper towels and facial tissues. Tea towels and dishcloths work pretty much everywhere you'd use a paper towel, and you can employ newspaper for the truly gnarly messes. As for facial tissue, toilet tissue works just as well at a fraction of the cost and without separate packaging. Why buy something twice?

October 30:
Staying in Touch Is Good for Everybody

Physical touch is essential for the physical, psychological, and emotional health of human beings. Massage in particular has been shown to help fight depression, decrease blood pressure and cortisol levels, and boost white blood cell counts. It's safe, all natural, and even a lovely way to care for a friend who is ailing. Best-case scenario—trade massages!

October 31:
Happy Halloween!

Bowl of candy? Check. Costume on? Check. Pumpkins carved? Check. Today is All Hallow's Eve and what better day is there to dress up, go out, and overindulge on sugary sweets? However, take a few precautions before venturing out:

- If you have kids, don't let them trick-or-treat without supervision.
- Don't let your child eat candy that doesn't come in a wrapper.
- Hold a flashlight when outside so drivers can see you.

But Halloween doesn't have to be all about the sugar rush and crazy costumes. It can also be a very charitable day:

- Make cards of kindness.
- Some children are too ill to go out trick or treating. Make homemade Halloween cards for hospitalized children with life-threatening illnesses and mail to either Love Letters: Random Cards of

Kindness (loveletterscares.org) or Hugs and Hope (hugsandhope.org).

- Many dentists' offices participate in post-Halloween candy buybacks. Donated sweets are sent to organizations such as Operation Gratitude (operationgratitude.com) or Operation Shoebox (operationshoebox.com). Both organizations include the candy in care packages for US soldiers in harm's way. Find a participating dental office near you at halloweencandybuyback.com.

chapter eleven

November

Gratitude and Giving Go Hand-in-Hand

This is what the heart knows beyond all words...a magnificent light surrounds us, more than anyone could ask for. This is what prayer as gratitude can open us up to.

—MARK NEPO

November 1:
A Plate of Cookies Can Change a Life

You know how sometimes certain memories remain crystal clear as though they are trapped in the amber of your consciousness? While I don't know nearly enough about how the brain works, I suspect these shards of memory that stay with us are some of the most important events of our lives to be pondered upon for all that they contain. They might be teachable moments for us to draw upon. While the neuroscience aspects elude me, I do know this memory is a life lesson:

My besties and I like to have a cup of tea now and again, the fancy kind with tea cakes, cupcakes, and cookies that are almost too beautiful to eat. During my decade in the Lower Haight, my dear friends and I got together once a month, taking turns at each other's houses. I was excited to be hosting one lovely late spring day and planned everything to the tee—lemon bars with lime icing, mini-cupcakes with icing that looked like lace, and my favorite black and white cookies, chocolate on one side and vanilla on the other. I even had brightly colored paper napkins with sassy wild women quotes on them.

I was working in Berkeley and living in San Francisco,

which meant that just getting across the Bay Bridge was going to be an adventure. On this day, it was going to be a miracle. I was terrified my friends would be standing at the front door, stamping their nicely shod feet, waiting for me as I navigated the traffic. I surrendered to it, knowing my anxiety would not change a thing. Plus, I had my secret weapon—the nicest array of confections ever. How could they be mad at me when they were being served stunningly beautiful cookies on napkins that reminded them they are fabulous?

Finally, my lane of traffic oozed off the Fremont exit into downtown San Francisco. I was going to bust one of my special moves and drive down a one-way arterial to avoid the clogged streets. To do that, I had to drive past the Transbay Terminal, one of the most desolate and derelict spots in all of the greater Bay Area. I was chugging along and feeling good about my bag of goodies, when I was stopped again by a Muni bus that appeared to be lumbering along at maybe three miles per hour. But I still had my special treats and my confidence remained intact.

I looked to my left and a mother and her toddler were standing on the raised median about two feet away from my car. She looked to be not much older than a teenager herself, and had a big bruise on her cheek and a frightened look. Her little boy was hugging her knee, trying to stay warm in the arctic wind that blasts San Francisco as soon as the sun sets. I smiled at them and she smiled back, and I saw then she was missing at least one tooth. In this moment, I just knew she had run away from an abusive home and was getting herself and her son to safety. I also knew in that moment that they needed money. I scrambled around in my messy purse but could only find a five-dollar bill, as I had spent all my cash on the sweets. I grabbed the pretty paper bag filled with boxes of delicacies and shoved it into her hands along with the wadded up bill. The look on her face was what will stay with me a lifetime. She was surprised, and the stress drained out of her face and I could see how pretty she was. The bus shot forward and I had to drive away but I managed to shout back at her, "These are the best cookies in the world, so everything is going to be ok!" I looked in the rearview mirror and saw her bend down. She opened a box and lovingly fed her little boy one of my treasured black and whites. They were laughing and her son was even dancing around. My heart lifted as I drove away. I was especially pleased that this young woman was going to be reminded about her fabulousness by sassy paper napkins.

My girlfriends and I ate microwaved popcorn that night but nobody minded. We also ended up having a much deeper and richer discussion about real things, no shop or shopping talk, no boyfriend problems. We talked about how lucky we were and ways we could give back to the world.

It is funny how I knew those cookies were going to save the night. I guess I just didn't know whose.

November 2:
An Extra Hour to Do Lots of Good

When you turn your clocks back one hour for daylight savings, make sure to spend that extra hour doing something productive. This is like a second chance at tackling the day. What did you need to get done yesterday that you didn't? Here is one great way to spend that hour: cruise over to myphilanthropedia.org to find your perfect match of an organization to donate to or volunteer with. I learned about this website from a TED Talk and discovered this vital service. Philanthropedia rates verified, financially responsible charities according to how much great work they're doing. Today, 3,121 experts have participated in Philanthropedia's research, providing reviews on 767 top nonprofits across 36 causes. I have bookmarked this on my desktop and check in often.

November 3:
Make It Count

My boyfriend is first-generation American Chinese, an "ABC." His family was unable to vote or even own property until the Civil Rights Act was passed in the sixties. He tells his children to "make it count" and passionately follows local, national, and international events and politics. Get educated about the governance of your own neighborhood in addition to the national political landscape. Exercise your right to vote. Voting is a sacred right that is one of the most important parts of our political system. Be informed about what is going on in your country, know what ideas you support and are against, and vote on each Election Day to speak for the public—you will be heard.

November 4:
Write Letters and Send Postcards

The things that make me the happiest have emotional and physical effects. These effects are felt even more when they are done for someone else. One of the most lasting is writing a personal letter. Born in the transitional time between letters and computers, many people in my generation have already shunned snail mail as a way to communicate. This makes letters rare, but a very inexpensive surprise. My grandmother was one of seven children, and they communicated with a round-robin letter. From mailbox to mailbox, they would add an update on their life and send it around to the next sibling. She taught me that letters are a valuable form of communication, something she's emphasized as her memory slowly fades. I got into the habit of writing letters and during the times where I was most stressed, I would write a letter. Letters live somewhere between thoughts and stories. They are confidential and a piece of yourself that you can choose to scrap or share.

When I receive a letter, especially from someone whom I haven't heard from in awhile, I get a rush of endorphins, because I'm holding proof that the friend thought of me.

It's the same rush I get when someone is considerate or goes out of their way to help me. Most friends reciprocate with a call to say how happy they were to open a personal note rather than another bill.

I studied epistolary literature in college, often using my break from studying as a chance to write letters. Perhaps letters will go the way of Wells Fargo wagons, but I'll single-handedly support the post office as long as my friends have addresses and my fingers can write. Letters are my personal therapy, my rush of endorphins, my connection with those I love, and my alone time—my regular serving of happiness.

November 5:
What People Really Need

Much of the time, kindness is good common sense. Just think about what people really need. In low-income families with no other options, an infant can spend the entire day wearing the same diaper. Due to a lack of funds, some parents cannot afford to change their baby's diaper more than once a day, and most laundromats do not allow cloth diapers to be washed in their machines. Help out a family in need to cover the basics by donating diapers through the Diaper Bank Network at diaperbanknetwork.org.

November 6:
Seek Out the Shy

Rescue a wallflower. Most people know what it's like to go to a party and end up standing by yourself. If you see someone alone, mosey on over to them and strike up a conversation. Nine times out of ten, they will have the *most* interesting things to say out of anybody at the party or dance.

November 7:
Learn the Language of Kindness

Teach the English language...abroad! With programs all over the world, you can choose which country you want to teach in. Often, housing is provided by a host family—or you can live on your own. Usually prior teaching experience is not required, though you can earn a certificate in Teaching English as a Foreign Language (TEFL). Visit interexchange.org for more information.

November 8:
Look at Everything in a New Way

Simply reframe your perception: each of us has had dreams that for one reason or another, we do not achieve. And we may have made choices that perhaps were not the best. Yet, rather than allowing regret to overtake us, we must celebrate all the other goals we've accomplished and positive choices we've made.

Human nature so often leads us to perceive the one negative in a sea of positives. But we can retrain ourselves to learn the lessons embedded in our mistakes, and allow ourselves to feel pride in the beauty we are capable of. All it takes is a little shift. You'll see.

November 9:
Make Time for Gratitude Every Day

When we begin a daily practice of recognizing the positive events that occur and the pleasant encounters we have with others, we will start being more thankful as the days pass. Perhaps it's someone who holds the door for you at the supermarket, the nice conversation you have with a stranger while at the coffee shop, or a hug with someone you love. These are the small moments, and often the ones we forget. Savor their beauty and what they tell you about humankind—that we do live among many good people.

November 10:
Shower the People You Love with Love

After a wedding or party, donate all of the flowers to a nursing home or hospital. Alternately, take them to your place of work and fill the entire office with beauty and love.

November 11:
Your Friends from the Farm

Gene and Lorri Bauston found a living sheep abandoned on a stockyard "dead pile" in 1986. Once they recovered from the shock, they rescued the sheep, named her Hilda, and went to work creating the Farm Sanctuary. Within ten years, Farm Sanctuary became the nation's largest farm animal rescue and protection organization. They now have a New York shelter and one in California, 100 miles north of Sacramento. Their website is farmsanctuary.org. Not only does their organization rescue thousands of farm animals each year, but they are also involved in groundbreaking campaigns to help animals. Another way you can support this effort is to visit a sanctuary with your kids, as they often include quaint petting zoos with fuzzy critters!

November 12:
Give an Hour of Your Time

Talk to United States troops. Give An Hour (giveanhour. org) is a nonprofit organization that provides free counseling to soldiers returning from Iraq and Afghanistan, including their families. This is a great way to show your support to the military while making space for needed mental health services.

November 13:
The Needs of the Many
Outweigh the Needs of the Few

Use Goodsearch.com to search the Internet, play games, or answer survey questions. This for-profit company donates a portion of all advertising revenue to charity (50% of revenue or one cent for each search).

November 14:
Good Karma

Holding the elevator: a simple yet kind idea. If you are inside of an elevator and see someone approaching as the doors close, hold the doors open to let them in. You might make a nice connection and the person will appreciate this gesture. Rack up those karma points!

November 15:
America Recycles Day

According to 50 Ways to Help the Planet (50waystohelp.com), "Recycled glass reduces related air pollution by 20% and related water pollution by 50%. If it isn't recycled it can take a million years to decompose.... 20 recycled aluminum cans could be made with the energy it takes to manufacture one brand new one. Every ton of glass recycled saves the equivalent of nine gallons of fuel oil needed to make glass from virgin materials."

November 16:
Muchas Gracias

· · · · · · · · · · · ·

I learned from my globetrotting friend Santosh that one of the nicest things a traveler can do is to learn how to say the basics in the language of the locals. He stressed that saying "thank you" is the *most* important phrase of all. His guide to global gratitude is below:

Arabic: Shukran

Czech: Děkuji

Danish: Tak

Dutch: Dank u

Estonian: Tänan teid

Filipino: Salamat

Finnish: Kiitos

French: Merci

German: Danke

Hungarian: Köszönöm

Indonesian: Terima kasih

Irish: Go raibh maith agat

Italian: Grazie

Japanese: Arigato

Latvian: Paldies

Norwegian: Takk

Polish: Dziękuję

Portuguese: Obrigado

Romanian: Mulţumesc

Spanish: Gracias

Swahili: Asante

Swedish: Tack

Vietnamese: Cảm ơn bạn

Welsh: Diolch yn fawr

November 17:
How to Have an Attitude of Gratitude

1. Be grateful and recognize the things others have done to help you.

2. When you say, "Thank you," to someone, it signals what you appreciate and why you appreciate it.

3. Post a "Thank you to all" on your Facebook page or your blog, or send individual emails to friends, family, and colleagues.

4. Send a handwritten thank-you note. These are noteworthy because so few of us take time to write and mail them.

5. Think thoughts of gratitude—two or three good

things that happened today—and notice calm settle through your head, at least for a moment. It activates a part of the brain that floods the body with endorphins, or feel-good hormones.

6. Remember the ways your life has been made easier or better because of others' efforts. Be aware of and acknowledge the good things, large and small, going on around you.

7. Keep a gratitude journal to list the people or things you're grateful for today. The list may start out short, but it will grow as you notice more of the good things around you.

8. Being grateful shakes you out of self-absorption and helps you recognize those who've done wonderful things for you. Expressing that gratitude continues to draw those people into your sphere.

9. Remember this thought from Maya Angelou: "When you learn, teach; when you get, give."

10. Join forces to do good. If you have survived illness or loss, you may want to reach out to others to help as a way of showing gratitude for those who reached out to you.

November 18:
Pass Along Self-Esteem

Donate "once in a lifetime" clothing such as old brides-maid dresses or even your wedding dress. Many people cannot afford formalwear for special events and if we are done wearing them, why keep them? Keep your own memories alive through pictures, and pass the dress or suit along to make someone feel happy and special for their own big moment.

Author and all-around-good-person Lara Starr offered this tip: "I'm a huge fan of Image for Success and the work they do in San Rafael, California. Image for Success provides men and women who are transitioning to work with two-week professional and casual wardrobes so they can embark on their new lives feeling like a million bucks! Clothes and how we present ourselves can have a huge impact on our self-esteem,. Giving these folks the time, attention, and resources to look and feel their best means the world. And the thrift shop Image for Success runs is one of my favorite places to shop. The staff and volunteers always make shopping fun! Their tidy shop with well-chosen, quality items is a great place to score designer finds on the cheap!" Visit the website at imageforsuccess.org.

November 19:
A Fantastic Warm-Up Act

Warm Up America (warmupAmerica.org) works with community service organizations and the American Red Cross to distribute warm, handmade blankets to those who need them. Warm Up America volunteers are encouraged to donate their finished blankets to a local organization (or a local chapter of a national organization) near where they live or work. My family collects old blankets and my mom's best friend is a master quilter who can make a gorgeous patchwork blanket that would keep anyone quite cozy for years to come. Staying warm can be a beautiful thing!

November 20:
Universal Children's Day

Today we should all make a greater effort to support the welfare of the children of the world. Participate in a charity, organization, or activity that promotes the welfare of children such as Save the Children, UNICEF, Global Movement for Children, Childreach International, Children's Defense Fund, and any others you may find.

"We were all children once. And we all share the desire for the well-being of our children, which has always been and will continue to be the most universally cherished aspiration of humankind."

—WE THE CHILDREN,
AT THE WORLD SUMMIT FOR CHILDREN
REPORT OF THE SECRETARY-GENERAL

November 21:
It Takes a Village and *You*

In early 2010, in the small village of Nshupu, Tanzania, nine malnourished orphans were sleeping on a cement floor without even a blanket or sufficient food. Four years later, these children have a lovely new permanent home, are attending school, and have welcomed six more orphans to their family. Their home also serves as a village community center that hosts, among other things, a weekly women's empowerment group that has created a savings and loan program for impoverished single mothers and widows. There is also a kindergarten program that serves 70 village children annually, including feeding them regular meals. All these endeavors are shepherded by PreciousProject.org, which explains on their website,

"Though lack of education is a leading cause of poverty, Tanzanian schools are not free. Attendance even at the primary school level requires the ability to pay for school uniforms, meals, materials, equipment, fees, and other expenses. As a result, there are children who are unable to even receive a primary education. Our goal is to help break the cycle of poverty by providing educational opportunities for orphans and other high-risk children."

November 22:
Knitting the World Back Together with a Lot of Love

Volunteer was never a word in her vocabulary. Not that Lee Gant didn't know what it meant, but it wasn't something she would ever think about doing. Feeling unloved as a child left her self-centered, angry, and needy. As far as Lee was concerned, the world owed her. But it was hard to get to know the world, as small as hers was. Sheltered and sequestered in a small coastal community in rural New England, she knew little about the daily lives of regular people with regular families, but enough to know that hers wasn't like theirs. "Bad things happened in my house," she said, "and I never understood why, because I was afraid to ask."

Throughout her teen and young adult years, Lee used drugs and alcohol to transport herself, begging attention from anyone and everyone. Chemicals seemed to work in the short haul, but eventually they led to more destructive behaviors: setting fires, shoplifting, drunk driving, punching through plate glass windows. Cutting helped drain her pent up self-loathing and relieved her. Sutures and butterfly bandages briefly put her back together, but after so many years and so many scars, self-mutilation wasn't working. After three weeks in an institution for attempted suicide, she was ready to try something different.

One day, out of the blue, Lee was invited into a knit shop filled with happy, loving people and found a passion and joy she never knew before. "I made things with my hands and felt good about myself. I entered an afghan in the county fair and won a blue ribbon. I joined AA and stopped drinking. I found a community of creative people who accepted me and my knitting and that, along with sober living, brought the attention I craved. But still...something was missing," she said. She noticed she felt best when she shared her knowledge of knitting and making other people happy brought a new kind of satisfaction.

On a whim, Lee volunteered to teach knitting classes for kids for the local Santa Rosa chapter of Catholic
Charities (CatholicCharities.org) She wanted to find out
if knitting would make a difference for them like it did
for her. She wanted to give them something they could
turn to when life got too scary, or complicated, or boring...something they could turn to for comfort or fun.
She gave them sticks and string and direction. She gave
them an opportunity to feel accomplished and proud. She
gave them a piece of herself and found what she'd been
missing.

Lee began to care about other people. "I taught families at a homeless shelter to knit. I taught a group of foster
teens. I crocheted for battered women and premature babies. I knitted warm hats for cold-headed cancer patients
I would never get to know.

"All of this giving changes me. I feel good inside. No
longer hollow and self-centered, I feel something akin to
love. For others. For myself. For who I am. For what I
do." Lee is not just any knitter; she is tremendously gifted
and tremendously generous. She is the author of several
books, including *Love in Every Stitch,* and is a sought-
after pattern designer. Go to her Facebook page, "Knit-

ting and Healing With Lee Gant," or you can find her at a shelter with a lot of bright, beautiful skeins of yarn and a bunch of happy kids, doing what she does best.

I asked Lee to sum up how it was that she came to "be a good in the world."

"I blame it on volunteering," she said.

November 23:
From Growing Up Homeless to Helping the Homeless

NFL player James Jones knows it's better to give than to receive. "Being homeless made me a better man," says James Jones, wide receiver for the Oakland Raiders since 2014. "And while I wouldn't wish anyone to go through that, I wouldn't change anything as far as how I grew up." Having slept in shelters and on park benches for the first 15 years of his life, Jones' success as an athlete defies stereotypes about homelessness and poverty.

He has taken his challenging experiences to heart. Since being drafted to the NFL in 2007, he has volunteered for many community organizations, and in 2008, started his own with his wife, Tamika. The Love Jones 4 Kids foundation (lovejones4kids.com) provides funding for school supplies, football camps, and pep talks to underprivileged children, many of them living in the same conditions that Jones did growing up.

"People are used to hearing about a homeless person or kid and don't think it's possible to be a professional football player. But down on your luck doesn't mean down and out." Touchdown!

November 24:
A Major Gender Justice Superhero

Staffed entirely by transgender folks, the TGI Justice Project (tgijp.org) has been dedicated to supporting transgender people both inside and outside of prison since 2003. Devoted to forging "a culture of resistance and resilience to strengthen us for the fight against imprisonment, police violence, racism, poverty, and societal pressures," TGIJP answers prison letters from transgender, gender non-conforming, and intersex prisoners. It also provides resources, funding, and support to low-income transgender women of color who are in prison, formerly incarcerated, or targeted by the police, and their families.

Helmed by Executive Director Miss Major, the legendary transgender rights advocate who has been an activist since before the Stonewall Riots of 1969, the TGI

Justice Project describes itself as seeking to "create a world rooted in self determination, freedom of expression, and gender justice."

November 25:
Free First Aid

When tragedies happen, it is often hard to know what to do. Here is a shining example of a positive reaction. When police refused to call an ambulance soon enough to save the fatally wounded Oscar Grant in 2009, Sharena Thomas and Lesley Phillips decided that too many people lacked knowledge of even the most basic emergency first aid techniques. Together, these Occupy activists founded the People's Community Medics, and since 2012 they have been providing free first aid training and first aid materials to Bay Area residents.

Their website, peoplescommunitymedics.org, explains, "This project is an act of self determination. We resist the state's disregard for our well being and are creating an alternative reality. We hope that one day every child will be taught basic first aid in school."

Committed to teaching their community how to treat medical emergencies in the absence of an ambulance,

Thomas and Phillips call their project "a people centered alternative" to institutional support that often is unreliable in its response to low-income communities and communities of color.

November 26:
Thanksgiving: Count Your Blessings

Thanksgiving Day brings families and friends together in a celebration of gratitude and thanks. However, it is also a time for reflection and for giving back to your community and to those less fortunate. Millions of people across America and the world could use a little helping hand. One good group to volunteer with and donate to is Convoy of Hope. Their mission ranges from providing disaster reponse, supporting local farmers, and feeding the hungry, to signature events with grocery give-aways, job-placement assistance, and health screenings. Go to convoyofhope.org and find out what you can do to help.

November 27:
Make Someone Happy!

As the old Jimmy Durante song goes, "make someone happy." A thoughtful, hand-written letter will do that *every time*! If you make just one someone happy, you will be happy, too.

November 28:
National Day of Listening

Be an active listener. When someone else is speaking, it is easy to become distracted by thoughts and external sounds, such a car horn or other nearby conversations—and by giving in to these distractions you can miss crucial details from the speaker. Let the person who is talking know that you are listening by making eye contact and focusing on the sound of their voice rather than the distractions around you. Additionally, don't interrupt someone when they are speaking. Listen, then respond. Quite often, people are not looking to be "fixed"—they truly just want to be heard.

November 29:
You Don't Have to Adopt to Make an Impact

Adopting an animal is a serious commitment. For those who aren't able to adopt, but still want to make a difference in the life of an abandoned animal, fostering is an excellent alternative.

There are many foster programs that give cat- and dog-lovers the chance to provide interim housing for displaced pets who have yet to find their forever home. Many of these foster programs cover food and medical expenses, meaning all you have to worry about is giving your furry guest a safe and loving play to stay. And who knows? You might just fall in love.

November 30:
Fighting Illiteracy One Book at a Time

I keep seeing these charming itty bitty libraries in my neighborhood, where you can take a book or give one in return. Some are plain serviceable boxes somewhat like a birdhouse for books and some are very ornate, not unlike something you might find in the upscale sections of the Shire. The organization Little Free Library (LittleFreeLibrary.org) describes their mission this way:

It's a "take a book, return a book" gathering place where neighbors share their favorite literature and stories. In its most basic form, a Little Free Library is a box full of books where anyone may stop by and pick up a book (or two) and bring back another book to share. You can, too!

chapter twelve

December

The Season of Giving

Live each day as if it were a gift. And, actually, it is.

—NINA LESOWITZ

December 1:
World AIDS Day

HIV, the virus that causes AIDS, has become one of the world's most serious health and developmental challenges. In the United States alone, 1.7 million people are estimated to have the HIV virus. According to aids.gov, 33.4 million people are living with the HIV/AIDS virus globally and more than 25 million deaths resulted in the virus worldwide since the first reported cases in 1981. Educate yourself and your family about this epidemic, promote safe behavior, and consider volunteering some of your time toward helping those infected.

AmfAR's "Countdown to a Cure for AIDS" is a research initiative aimed at finding a broadly applicable cure for HIV by 2020. "Countdown to a Cure" is designed to intensify amfAR's (amFar.org) cure-focused HIV research program with plans to strategically invest $100 million in cure research over the next six years.

December 2:
Have a Do-It-Yourself Christmas, so Start Crafting Now!

Make your Christmas presents this year. It's more personal and will save you money. From a tin of homemade fudge to a colorful knitted scarf, your family and friends are sure to appreciate your hard work and thoughtfulness. You can also think bigger! Knit, sew, and quilt your way to a better world with the organizations below:

- The Mother Bear Project gives hand-knit and crocheted bears to children affected by HIV/AIDS in emerging nations so they know that they are loved. (motherbearproject.org)

- Socks For Soldiers knits socks for those on active duty serving in the Middle East. (socksforsoldiersinc.com)

- Stitching Up the World knits, crochets, and sews items to donate to chemotherapy patients, Special Olympic athletes, and others in New Hampshire. (candiawomansgroup.org/stitching/index.html)

- Threads of Love provides clothing, blankets, and other handmade articles for premature and sick infants. Threads of Love has chapters in the United States, Canada and London, England. (threadsoflove.org)

● Tiny Stitches is based in Gwinnett County, Georgia and provides basic layettes to disadvantaged newborns in north Georgia. They also provide burial ensembles to families who lose an infant. (tinystitches.org)

December 3:
Operation Christmas Child

Make Christmas special for boys and girls around the world by packing a shoebox with new toys, school supplies, and socks. Go to samaritanspurse.org/operation-christmas-child/pack-a-shoe-box for more information on how to pack a box. You can choose the gender and age group for your donation, and you can even track the box to see where it ends up! For even more packing ideas, check out: faithfulprovisions.com/2012/10/01/101-operation-christmas-child-shoebox-ideas.

December 4:
Giving a Gift of Sustainability
· · · · · · · · · · · ·

Have a friend or loved one that wants something unique for Christmas? Visit heifer.org to view and purchase some of the most helpful and generous gifts that can be given—but they don't fit in a box and they won't arrive on your friend's doorstep.

Heifer International is an organization that works with communities to end hunger and poverty by providing sustainable agriculture and animals to families in need. You can "purchase" a goat for $120, a flock of geese for $20, a hope basket for $50, or browse the website for other options. These gifts are priceless (figuratively) and won't go unappreciated or unused. Think about the positive impact you can make on family—a world of difference, actually!

December 5:
A Golden Ticket

Not many things will ruin your day quite like getting pulled over by the police. But when police in Lowell, Michigan, recently stopped 50 drivers for minor violations, the surprised motorists wound up getting their Christmas wishes instead of traffic tickets. Officer Scot VanSolkema chatted with the not-so-happy drivers, asking what they or their kids wanted for Christmas. Unbeknownst to anyone else, his buddies waited in a nearby shop, listening via radio before rushing to buy, wrap, and deliver whatever the drivers had named, including toys, an Xbox, and a high-definition TV. Said one happy driver: "This just turned my bad day into a good one."

December 6:
People Are Resources, Too

Make plans to go to a local nursing home and visit an elderly resident who hasn't gotten a visitor lately. Receiving extra one-on-one attention can be very rewarding for the resident and you'll be surprised how interesting their life is once you start talking with them. Especially with the holidays coming, think of those who might not have family nearby who would love good company at this time of year. Nine times out of ten, you will end up receiving much more than you give to these elders, who have wisdom, stories, advice, and love to offer.

December 7:
Random Acts of Roses

Use your flower power: go to your local discount store and pick up some small vases. Add a ribbon, some freshly picked flowers, and deliver the arrangements to elders at a local community center, nurses in the ER, or anywhere you know people can use little random acts of roses.

December 8:
Charity Rocks!

When Jaime Finkel, assistant to music manager Scott Rodger, began working at Maverick in Beverly Hills, she noticed that there was a lot of unclaimed "merch" in the office. The newly-formed company, which is composed of nine of music's top managers—who collectively manage more than two dozen of the planet's biggest artists, including Madonna, Paul McCartney, Miley Cyrus, Pharrell Williams, Alicia Keys, Arcade Fire, and U2—is at the forefront of major changes taking place in the music industry today.

Instead of throwing away the excess and unwanted tour products and unsolicited gifts, Jaime initiated a Merch Box. Every month, she selects an organization to donate these items to. It seems like a natural match since for every celebrity and wanna-be star in Hollywood there is a person in need, but no one had thought to do this before. It's as simple as setting up a bin in your office lunchroom and creating a sign that reads "For Charity."

December 9:
Support Diversity in Education

New York-based Folk Arts Rajasthan (folkartsrajasthan. org) and India-based Lok Kala Sagar Sansthan (LKSS)— meaning "local folk arts society"—are nonprofit organizations joined since 2005 by a shared vision of a thriving and just future for the Merasi people and their unique musical culture. The Merasi of northwestern India carry a powerful legacy of 38 generations but they also carry the burden of the still-enduring caste system. To reclaim an identity as storytellers, the Merasi of Jaisalmer have shed the derogatory caste label *Manganiya*r, meaning beggars. The name *Merasi* instead means musicians, and is a symbol of self-determination.

The FAR-LKSS collaborative approach recognizes that education, preserving this intangible cultural heritage, and achieving social justice for a continually marginalized people are mutually dependent goals.

In the face of obstinate hierarchical norms, FAR and LKSS are together nurturing a generation of ambitious and capable youth with their programs. Significantly, two FAR scholarship girls, Sitara and Mobeena Khan, participated in a 2014 US-based international science conference, after their project won awards at both local and state level in Rajasthan. In February 2015, a troupe of Merasi youth traveled to Mumbai to play in the prestigious Kala Ghoda Arts Festival and exchange cultural activities with students at a variety of schools.

December 10:
Human Rights Day

Today presents an opportunity to celebrate human rights and advocate for equal human rights everywhere. As much as we like to think that the world is all sunshine and rainbows, that is not the truth; we should not be blind or ignorant to the truth. Today, make yourself aware of the injustices going on in the world by doing some research on the prejudices and hate that many people experience from others. Do what you can to help promote human rights today and everyday. To keep up on all the latest, check out hrw.org.

December 11:
Save the Planet, One Tree at a Time
· · · · · · · · · · · ·

Buy an artificial Christmas tree. People love my blue and silver disco tree which I got at yard sale a few years ago. It is *very* festive! On average, over 30 million Christmas trees are sold in the United States each year—those are trees we could be saving and using for oxygen, housing material, and paper products rather than as decoration for a small amount of time. When you purchase an artificial tree, you will save money within the first few years and they look just as nice without the mess of pine needles! For more information on the history of the Christmas tree, go to urbanext.illinois.edu/trees/facts.cfm.

December 12:
Make Merry
· · · · · · · · · · · ·

Santa Claus came early to a Pennsylvania retailer recently. In December 2014, an anonymous man walked into a store and told the manager he wanted to donate $50,000 to help pay off customer layaway accounts. "We made him say it twice," said store manager Steve Meyers. "When we started calling customers, they thought it might be a joke."

The donor, who asked to be known only as Santa B., arrived just in time, as unfulfilled layaway orders were set to be cancelled that day. "He just wanted to bring Christmas cheer to everyone," Meyers said. "He was in and out, kind of like Santa Claus."

December 13:
Ring Your Bells

"Ring bells and help raise money for people in need. The Red Kettle Christmas Campaign enables the Salvation Army to provide food, toys and clothing to over six million people during the Christmas season and helps more than 34 million Americans recovering from all kinds of personal disasters nationwide. The Red Kettle campaign, first started in San Francisco in 1891, has traditionally been the Salvation Army's most prominent fund-raiser." For more information and to find out where you can volunteer, go to ringbells.org.

December 14:
Be a Hospice Volunteer

Jollytologist Allen Klein shares this beautiful story:

When I was a hospice volunteer, one of the patients I was assigned to look after was an elderly woman who loved classical music. For many years, she, her son, and her daughter had season symphony tickets. But she was way too ill to use them now. Her prognosis was only a few weeks left to live.

I discussed the situation with the hospice team and how we might get her to a concert. Perhaps we could put her in a wheelchair or even put her on a gurney and have her at the back of the theater. But in her condition, we realized that that would not work.

Then I had an idea. I called the San Francisco Conservatory of Music, one of the leading music schools in the country, and asked if they had a student who might volunteer to play something for a dying woman. A few days later, they sent over a very talented young woman, a violinist, who gave a private performance for the patient and her family.

I wasn't at the apartment at the time but from what the daughter told me the next day, it was glorious. She said that after the intimate living room recital, her mother told her, "In all my years of going to the symphony, that was the best concert I have ever attended."

December 15:
Love Your Local Public Library

Libraries are just as much a community hub as any coffee house or breakfast joint. Your patronage will make a difference! Nowadays, libraries host events, offer free classes, and are a place we can go for some nice quiet time with a book or magazine. To me, they are as holy as shrines.

December 16:
Sign Up to Be Santa's Helper

Go to your local Post Office around Christmastime and pick one of the letters to Santa that they get every year. Buy and send the gift to the child who asked for it so the gift arrives before December 25.

December 17:
Actions Really Are Louder than Words

Pay attention to the body language of others around you. If you notice someone with droopy posture or a frown, offer assistance if they need it. That someone could be having a bad day, and one person noticing could make a big difference. Be that person.

December 18:
Host a Holiday Potluck

Since you might not get to see your close friends much in the next few days due to family gatherings, shopping for gifts, and getting over colds, invite them over for a holiday potluck. Spending time with friends is a great pick-me-up and now is a good time to show your gratitude for the people in your life. To make it even more fun, choose a theme for your party, such as tacky Christmas sweaters.

December 19:
The Red Cross Can Use More than Your Blood!

For some people, health, time, and logistical restraints mean donating blood isn't possible. But blood donation isn't the only way to support organizations like the Red Cross. Along with financial donations, the Red Cross also accepts airline miles and credit card rewards. Easily transferable from your computer, these sorts of donations don't cost anything but can still make a difference.

December 20:
If Something Really Worries You,
Do Something About It

Millions of tons of plastic waste litter the world's oceans, converging together in rotating currents called gyres and blanketing the water's surface. On average, these gyres now hold six times more plastic than plankton by dry weight. Fortunately, 19-year-old Boyan Slat, founder and president of the Ocean Cleanup (theoceancleanup.com), wanted to invent "a method to clean up almost half of the Great Pacific Garbage Patch in just 10 years, using currents." The youthful environmentalist and entrepreneur presented this revolutionary idea at a TEDx Talk in the Netherlands and was recently named one of Intel's 20 Most Promising Young Entrepreneurs Worldwide.

December 21:
Make Time to Make Memories

'Tis the season to... spend more time with those you love! Instead of sequestering yourselves in separate rooms watching television, playing video games, or browsing the Internet, call all family members into the same room and do something together. Play a board game, watch a movie, have everyone contribute to making dinner, then roast marshmallows in the fireplace. Or maybe chestnuts. Ho ho!

December 22:
Think Globally

Start a conversation with someone of a different culture, religion, or political view, while actively listening and responding. Becoming aware of someone else's standpoints and personal journeys may enlighten how you think.

Nowadays, people of different vantage points need to realize that we may worship differently but we are people all the same. Be accepting and show it. This time of year, so many different cultures celebrate the turn of the year in ways unique to their traditions. Why not find out more about these festivities and even attend some? It's a small world, after all, right?

December 23:
Happy Hanukkah!

The Jewish Festival of Lights begins this time of year and has a marvelous tradition of giving, known as *tzedakah*. When translated into English, tzedakah means charity—giving to those in need. Derived from the Hebrew word *tzade-dalet-qof*, meaning righteous or fair, this practice of giving is both a generous act and a just one in the Jewish religion. In Jewish literature, the sages have said that

this performance of duty is equal to all other command-
ments combined. Tzedakah is what grants us forgiveness
from our sins.

Certain kinds of tzedakah are considered to be of
greater merit than others. Maimonides organized the different tzedakah into a hierarchical list. From the least to
most meritorious they are:

- Giving begrudgingly
- Giving less than you should, but giving cheerfully
- Giving after being asked
- Giving before being asked
- Giving when you are unaware of the recipient's
  identity, but the recipient is aware of yours
- Giving when you are aware of the recipient's iden-
  tity, yet you remain anonymous
- Giving when neither party is aware of the other's
  identity
- Enabling the recipient to become self reliant

December 24:
Christmas Eve

As your family arrives—or as you arrive at your family's—to celebrate Christmas, greet everyone with a genuine smile and embrace. Leave any past disagreements at the door and see the good in everyone. You love these people and they love you. Bond over happy memories and the amazing dinner spread on the table.

December 25:
Share the Love

The holidays can be a difficult time for many people who don't have family nearby, a home to sleep in, or food to eat. A great way to be a good in the world is to volunteer a few hours of your time to work in a soup kitchen and help serve those who are in need of a hot meal. You can also use this time to get your family involved and impart good moral values on your children. For many years running, I have volunteered at Glide Memorial Church in downtown San Francisco and enjoyed each and every minute of it. I bet your community has a place like Glide that can be your happy place. Make other people happy and feel your own special joy. If you find yourself in the

San Francisco Bay Area around Thanksgiving or Christmas, check out glide.org/serveameal, then come on down and we'll have fun together serving up some love.

The Volunteer Resource Program at Glide works with about 10,000 volunteers each year, totaling 65,000 hours of service. The Glide Meals Program is a transformative experience. This program requires 85 volunteers each day to fill the breakfast, prep, lunch and dinner shifts, all 365 days a year. With your help they can serve up to 2,400 meals per day to the Glide community. Volunteers assist with everything from serving food, to bussing tables, to handing out silverware and condiments. Be prepared to roll up your sleeves, and make some beautiful human connections!

December 26:
Re-Gifting 101

Now that you and your family have celebrated, eaten to your heart's content, and opened presents, ask if everyone likes their gifts and if they will use them. If there is something that doesn't fit or isn't useful, donate it. I remember when people were shocked that FLOTUS Nancy Reagan re-gifted but I think she was just ahead of the curve!

If your heart and your wallet have different ideas about making monetary donations, it is time to summon your inner re-gifter. An unwanted gift could be a welcome donation to a charitable organization. For help selecting a charitable organization, visit the Better Business Bureau's Wise Giving Alliance at give.org. You can also contact the government office responsible for registering charities in your state. A little research upfront will make sure that your donation is put to good use. If the process of selecting a charity seems daunting, remember that you benefit from giving as well.

Involving your children in the selection of a charity teaches valuable lessons. You have an opportunity to make a difference. Some charitable gifts are tax-deductible if made to a qualified organization. But be sure your organization meets IRS guidelines, as there may be different tax breaks when you donate certain types of assets to charity.

December 27:
Reach Out

The holidays can be an intensely lonely time. I remember when I first arrived in San Francisco and really had nowhere to go. Kindly folks invited me to Thanksgiving and Christmas, and I made new friends, ate marvelous dinners, and was so grateful. I try to do the same now that I have a home I can share. Look around and see whom you can invite over. This is a lovely tradition among my group of friends and is, I truly believe, what the holidays are really supposed to be about.

December 29:
Have a Gratitude Circle

Instead of just another holiday party, have friends over and state what you are grateful for in the world and about each other. Take note!

December 30:
Terrific for Terra

If you are anything like me, this is the time of year you suddenly realize you don't have enough flutes and glassware to properly toast the New Year. Why add to the already burgeoning mounds of recycling or, God forbid, landfill? The cool company Refresh Glass (refreshglass. com) creates pretty and eco-efficient drinking glasses from rescued wine bottles. Cheers!

December 31:
New Year's Eve

Make a number of envelopes with "Emergency Midnight Kisses" written on the front and put a few Hershey's kisses inside. Scatter these around town or the shindig you are at and bring a smile to many faces as you ring in the New Year.

What Does a Kinder World Look Like to You?

In the hurly-burly of this busy world, simple kindness and goodness can get left behind in the rush to be first in line, to reach the top of the corporate ladder, and to have the most "likes." But what does it all mean at the end of the day? Isn't being a good person and making real contributions to the world more important than anything else?

In recent years, I have reflected on my childhood in the sylvan hills of West Virginia, where I was raised on a farm in accordance with the Golden Rule. When I first arrived in San Francisco—literally wearing a blue gingham dress—I could not get over the sophistication and urbanity of Northern California. I loved it but was *very* intimidated by the houses without front yards, the hair, the far-out fashions, the very manneredness of it all. I arrived with $500 in my pocket, thinking I could live on that for some months in San Francisco. (You can stop laughing now.) Once reality set in, I quickly realized I needed to make money just to keep a roof over my head from one month to the next. This set me on a path of worrying about the bottom line as I worked two jobs and did my best to keep the coffers somewhat filled. I did notice, though, that I was not the same happy-go-lucky gingham gal that had rolled in from the sticks in the mid-eighties.

After years of working for multi-national corporations, I had become a workaholic and worrywart. I had seized upon the goal to go global with my work. After much jockeying, many long hours, and doing whatever it took, I finally landed a job as a buyer for one of the world's largest import/export outfits. My duties entailed traveling the world and shopping—on somebody else's dime, mind you. I was thrilled and could not stop bragging to anyone that would listen about my new gig.

The big day arrived and I was ushered in to the office of the top boss to go over our itinerary, which included stops in India, mainland China, Taiwan, Hong Kong, Portugal, and Italy. When I was shown photos of the factories in China and India, I nearly fainted, but blurted out, "Those are children. Our products are being made by children? How can this be?" I distinctly remember having an out-of-body experience. I was horrified to hear my own voice shrilly continuing on, "All the products in India have to be spray lacquered. Where are the fans, and vents, and masks?" Suddenly, I realized my "dream job" was, in fact, a nightmare.

My boss, a former merchant marine who was tougher than any nail, coolly responded, "They feel they are lucky to have a job and so should you."

I could not help myself and so I responded, "These kids will be coughing up their lungs before they are ten years old. This just isn't right. No way am I exploiting children and neither should you."

I could hardly believe what was coming out of my mouth. Looking back, it is one of my proudest moments. This was when I was reminded of what really matters. I learned that the good teachings instilled in me by my family had taken root, even in the citified soil. From then on, I have become more conscious, day by day, of living a life based on values. I quit my job the next day, despite being scared to death of not having any income. I used my newfound vocal skills to talk my way into a job in publishing, and best of all, with a publishing house specializing in philosophy, spirituality, self-help, and the wisdom traditions of the world. They even had a tree-planting program to offset the environmental impact.

At the end of life, I feel sure that having lots of money, fancy cars, and real estate will not be nearly as important as how much love you give to the world. This realization was the inspiration for *Be a Good in the World*, which I view as 365 big, bold, beautiful acts of kindness.

My sincere hope is that this book inspires you to put in motion your own ideas for making a difference. Moreover, we would love to hear your ideas and I would love nothing better than to hear from you directly. I am really excited about how much good you will bring to our world.

With love and gratitude,

Brenda Knight
brenda.knight@gmail.com

Index